Date Due

BRODART, CO.   Cat. No. 23-233-003   Printed in U.S.A.

Critical Judicial Nominations and
Political Change

Critical Judicial Nominations and Political Change

THE IMPACT OF CLARENCE THOMAS

Christopher E. Smith

PRAEGER

Westport, Connecticut
London

Library of Congress Cataloging-in-Publication Data

Smith, Christopher E.
    Critical judicial nominations and political change : the impact of
Clarence Thomas / Christopher E. Smith.
        p. cm.
    Includes bibliographical references and index.
    ISBN 0–275–94567–7 (alk. paper)
    1. United States. Supreme Court—Officials and employees—
Selection and appointment. 2. Judges—United States—Selection and
appointment. 3. United States—Politics and government—1989-
4. Thomas, Clarence, 1948-   . I. Title.
KF8742.S57   1993
347.73′2634—dc20
[347.3073534]   93–15349

British Library Cataloguing in Publication Data is available.

Library of Congress Catalog Card Number: 93–15349
ISBN: 0–275–94567–7

First published in 1993

Praeger Publishers, 88 Post Road West, Westport, CT 06881
An imprint of Greenwood Publishing Group, Inc.

Printed in the United States of America

The paper used in this book complies with the
Permanent Paper Standard issued by the National
Information Standards Organization (Z39.48-1984).

10 9 8 7 6 5 4 3 2 1

For Roosevelt and Judi Jones

Contents

Preface

A major challenge facing judicial scholars is to analyze courts and law in proper relation to the American political system. The earliest scholarly traditions in law schools and in the public law subfield of political science treated law and judicial decisions as independent from politics. Law was regarded as a set of coherent rules for human behavior that advanced procedural fairness, protection of property rights, and other significant societal interests. Judges were viewed as wise decision makers who applied and extended legal principles in logical, methodical fashion. The advent of legal realism in the early twentieth century helped to sweep away the formalist facade from scholars' understanding of law, yet it took several additional decades for political scientists to fully integrate their analyses of courts into broader conceptual frameworks addressing the United States' political governing system as a whole.

Among contemporary scholars, there is broad recognition of the connections and interactions between the judicial branch and the other elements and actors of the political system. Myriad studies in recent decades have examined the role of interest groups in advancing their policy agendas through litigation, the politics of judicial selection, interbranch conflicts concerning the development and implementation of judicial policies, and other topics illustrating the inherently political nature of law and the judicial system. Despite the thorough illumination of the intimate connections between courts and politics, scholars must guard against a tendency to analyze judicial institutions in isolation or otherwise treat law and judicial processes as unique, freestanding objects of academic inquiry. Because judicial institutions employ distinctive language, processes, symbols, and structures, it can be relatively easy for an excessively "micro-level" research focus to obscure or omit important "macro-level" implications of judicial phenomena.

The foregoing observations on tendencies in judicial research are not intended to denigrate the fine work of many scholars who have literally transformed contemporary understandings about the judicial branch's place *within*, rather than *apart from*, the American political system. Instead, these comments merely serve as a reminder of the benefits to be gained from questioning, challenging, and theorizing anew about the connections between courts and influential developments affecting American society. By examining selected judicial nominations for the United States Supreme Court, this study endeavors to make a modest step toward reconceptualizing and reassessing the importance of judicial phenomena in contributing to significant political developments and policy trends. As the pages that follow will explain in greater detail, the underlying argument of this book is that certain Supreme Court nominations (which may or may not result in confirmed appointments), labeled here as "critical judicial nominations," serve as catalytic events for important changes in politics and public policy that were unintended and unanticipated by the political actors who initiated the nominations. Hopefully, if the argument is cogent and persuasive, the "critical judicial nomination" concept may provide a useful tool for classifying and analyzing the impact and importance of the Supreme Court nomination process.

The Law and Society Association graciously granted permission to use the data for Table 4-1 drawn from Richard E. Miller and Austin Sarat, "Grievances, Claims, and Disputes: Assessing the Adversary Culture," *Law and Society Review* 15 (1980–81): 544. Chapter 3 contains material that originally appeared in Christopher E. Smith and Scott P. Johnson, "The First-Term Performance of

Justice Clarence Thomas," *Judicature*, 76 (1993). The American Judicature Society generously granted permission for its use. Other material in Chapter 3 originally appeared as Christopher E. Smith, "Supreme Court Surprise: Justice Anthony Kennedy's Move Toward Moderation," *Oklahoma Law Review* 45 (1992): 459–76. This material appears by agreement with the Oklahoma Law Review. Some of the discussion in Chapter 4 appears by permission of the Ohio Northern University Law Review. It originally appeared as Christopher E. Smith, "Politics and Plausibility: Searching for the Truth about Anita Hill and Clarence Thomas," *Ohio Northern University Law Review* 19 (1993): 697-757.

I am grateful to my father, Robert L. Smith of Western Michigan University, for the original suggestion to develop a book-length treatment for my research on the nomination of Clarence Thomas to the Supreme Court. I am indebted to John Green of the University of Akron and Thomas Hensley of Kent State University for discussions that helped to refine my thinking about the topics discussed in this book. They bear no responsibility, however, for the manner in which I drew from their comments and suggestions to generate my own analysis and conclusions. My sometime coauthor, Scott P. Johnson of the Ohio State University, has generously permitted me to use our joint research on Justice Clarence Thomas's first term that comprises much of the discussion in Chapter 3. I received assistance from several people in gathering information: Gregory Caldeira of the Ohio State University; Jana Nestlerode of West Chester University; Bevan and Fran Smith; John Andrew Farbarik; and Judy Banks.

As always, I am grateful to my colleagues in the Political Science Department at the University of Akron for creating an environment conducive to research and writing. This project was assisted by a Summer Faculty Research Fellowship from the University of Akron's Research (Faculty Projects) Committee. Bonnie Ralston did her usual fine job in assisting with preparation of the manuscript.

My wife Charlotte applied her recently completed law school education to supply especially valuable contributions—and encouragement—for the development of the ideas that are contained in this book. Her support and patience continue to be integral components of whatever success I achieve with my research. My children, Alicia and Eric, exhibit patience and understanding beyond what should reasonably be expected of preschoolers. They also provide me with needed distractions when I am on the verge of becoming too consumed with my work.

This book is affectionately dedicated to two of my strongest supporters, Roosevelt and Judi Jones. In addition to being superb parents-in-law to me and grandparents to my children, they have always gone above and beyond the call of duty in reading and digesting my academic writings and encouraging me to write more. Although I have always enjoyed extraordinarily strong support from my family (and especially from my parents) for my career choices and my sometimes controversial research topics, few of my blood relatives can match the invaluable level of interest, concern, and encouragement exhibited by my in-laws.

Critical Judicial Nominations and Political Change

1

Critical Judicial Nominations

The U.S. Supreme Court is recognized by scholars and politicians as an influential institutional actor in American national politics. Although many members of the public cling to conceptions of courts as legal institutions separate from the world of politics,[1] if pressed, even naive citizens can recognize many examples of the generally acknowledged connections between the judicial branch and the political governing system. For example, the nation's highest court receives significant attention from the news media and the public when presidents nominate new justices. Supreme Court nominees sometimes become the central figures in partisan confirmation battles. Democrats and Republicans compete with each other for control of the White House and the U.S. Senate, in part, because these institutions determine which individuals will become the country's most influential judicial decision makers—those who shape public policy concerning abortion, criminal justice, and a variety of other important subjects.

Because the Supreme Court is such an important institution in the governing system, scholars seek to analyze the nature and importance of the Court's past and continuing role in shaping American society. In assessing the Court's impact on political developments, scholars have analyzed the Court's conflicts with other branches of government, its role as a policy initiator, and its

status as the revered legitimizer of other branches' decisions.[2]
Virtually every analysis begets reanalysis that challenges asserted
premises and conclusions about the Court's actual role and significance.[3] The quasi-dialectical nature of the academic enterprise
directed at the study of the Supreme Court has reinforced the
underlying recognition of the Court's importance as the literal and
symbolic pinnacle of one branch within the governing system.
However, the conflicting conclusions of this scholarship have also
left open to debate any firm conclusions about the Court's precise
impact on political developments. What is most important about
the Supreme Court? Is it the Court's institutional role? Is it the
Court's specific policy-shaping decisions? Is it individual justices
who make their mark on American history? Obviously such questions are not easy to answer, particularly because the currents of
history may change the Supreme Court's role, importance, and
impact.

The underlying theme of this book is that the identification and
analysis of one kind of pivotal judicial phenomenon, conceptual-
ized as "critical judicial nominations," adds an important dimen-
sion to scholars' efforts to analyze the Supreme Court's importance
for American society. As the following chapters disclose, critical
judicial nominations constitute an alternative focal point for analysis that may broaden understanding of the existing scholarly
research that has concentrated on the Court's institutional role,
judicial policy-making, and individual justices.

ANALYZING THE SUPREME COURT'S ROLE
AND IMPORTANCE

In attempting to understand the Supreme Court, scholars often
seek to develop classification schemes that will reduce the Court's
history into units that are useful for analytical purposes. For
example, one available unit for analysis is the tenure of each chief
justice. One might examine the Supreme Court's importance by
assessing the Court's actions and impact during the respective
tenures of each chief justice. Although the tenures of some chief

justices might be notable for specific developments, such as famous case decisions, the Court's impact on society will not be highly associated with chief justices' terms in office. Because significant changes in the Court's composition and influential external political developments occur independently of chief justices' length of service in office, many of the Supreme Court's important actions and consequences for society will overlap the terms in office of various chief justices. The tenures of specific chief justices may be highly instructive for analyzing the Court, because these chief justices led (or failed to lead) the Court in addressing controversial issues. As a general unit of analysis, however, chief justices' tenures are more convenient than important.

The most commonly applied and perhaps most useful classification scheme emphasizes the Court's role in the country's political development during clearly defined historical eras. In its broadest form, the Court's history is analyzed by dividing it into three general eras: (1) 1789–1865 (the Court's role in defining and expanding the powers of the institutions of the national government); (2) 1865–1937 (the Court's role in defining and impeding government regulation of economic and social welfare issues in an increasingly complex industrialized society); and (3) 1937–90s (the Court's role in defining the relationship between individuals and the government through decisions in civil liberties cases).[4] Political scientists have further refined and sharpened the focus of these periodic classifications by linking the Court's role and behavior with simultaneous developments in electoral politics. For example, Walter Dean Burnham has written that "[o]ne of the most important indicators of critical [partisan] realignment [among the American electorate] is the eruption of political controversy centering on the Supreme Court, as happened in the crises of the 1860s, 1890s, 1930s, and 1960s."[5] Thus, under this view of political history, the Supreme Court is not regarded as an agent of societal change. Instead, the Court is viewed by competing ideological interests as one focal point for controversy during the periodic eras of intense political conflict in which the nature and definition of the electorate's partisan alignments change significantly. Other scholars examine the Supreme Court's role in the aftermath of new partisan alignments and argue that the Court contributes to the legitimacy and acceptance of new policies initiated by the new governing coalition.[6] Again, the Supreme Court is viewed as a secondary institutional actor reacting to and modestly influencing political developments that are primarily generated by forces external to the judicial branch.

In the final analysis, perhaps scholarly approaches that treat the Supreme Court as a secondary institutional entity for important historical developments, rather than as a primary catalyst for political change, will provide the most accurate overview of the Court's role and impact within the governing system. However, these approaches appear to suffer from two specific weaknesses that may diminish the comprehensiveness of their analyses. First, an institutional focus may obscure or preclude recognition of the impact and importance of individuals and discrete events that potentially contribute to broad social or political consequences. By giving exclusive attention to the Supreme Court as an institutional entity, the importance of individual justices or specific historical events may be overlooked. Second, approaches that treat the Court as the object of controversies between ideological interests or as a mere endorser of completed political changes may neglect to recognize important judicial contributions to significant political developments; contributions that are overlooked or undervalued by analysts who study the Court as a single institutional entity. If these neglected aspects are indeed weaknesses in analyses of the Supreme Court's importance, perhaps an alternative approach emphasizing these elements would generate new insights about the importance of the judicial branch in political developments affecting American society. Such an alternative approach need not necessarily replace the established institutional analyses, but rather merely produce new and, hopefully, significant insights about how the Supreme Court's role in the political system should be more comprehensively analyzed and understood.

DISCRETE EVENTS AND INDIVIDUAL
JUSTICES AS CATALYSTS FOR CHANGE

The Supreme Court provides myriad individuals and discrete events, in the form of specific justices and case decisions respectively, that could provide the basis for examining an alternative analytical approach. Every individual justice has an impact on the Court's behavior by casting votes in case decisions, authoring opinions, and interacting with other justices in the process of deciding cases. Every case decision has an impact on the individual litigants involved, on the development of case precedent to be followed by lower courts, and perhaps on broad public policy developments. If one assessed whether these individuals (i.e., justices) and discrete events (i.e., case decisions) have a catalytic impact on significant developments in the political system, it would become clear that most justices and most case decisions are, from a long-term historical perspective, individually of modest import for the American governing system and society.

There are several reasons why a single justice is unlikely to be a catalyst for important political change. For example, because individual justices cast only one vote among nine decision makers, the addition of any one justice is generally unlikely to produce significant consequences for society. Moreover, although a new justice may cast pivotal, decisive votes in a closely divided Court, the justice's decisive impact is unlikely to be long lasting because subsequent personnel changes will alter the compositional mix of the Court and, in all likelihood, diminish the importance of any single justice. In addition, the particular outcomes determined by a specific justice usually will not alter the general decisional trends and societal impact of the Supreme Court during a particular era.

The example of Justice David Souter, a justice who influenced the outcomes in many cases during his first two terms, illustrates how unlikely it is for any single justice to be a catalyst for significant political change. Justice Souter was appointed to the Supreme Court in 1990 at a time when the justices were closely divided on a variety of controversial issues. During his first term,

Souter cast the decisive fifth vote that determined case outcomes in twelve of nineteen 5–4 decisions. Included among the cases effectively decided by Souter's vote were seven criminal justice decisions and two First Amendment decisions that undoubtedly would have been decided the other way if Souter's liberal predecessor, Justice William Brennan, had remained on the Court.[7] During Souter's second term, he was even more influential in determining outcomes in close cases. Souter cast the decisive fifth vote in thirteen of the fourteen 5–4 decisions during the 1991–92 term.[8]

Although Souter's immediate impact on case outcomes may imply that his appointment was a catalytic event for determining Supreme Court decision making, his presence on the Court actually had modest significance for the highest court's role and impact. Many of Souter's decisive votes, including the seven criminal justice and two First Amendment cases during the 1990 term, cemented conservative outcomes consistent with the general decisional trend of the justices in the aftermath of appointments by Presidents Reagan and Bush. Souter's first term interagreement rates show him to consistently join the other conservative justices. Interagreement rates show the percentage of decisions in which each justice agreed with each of his or her colleagues. Such rates are used as a measure of the like-mindedness of each pair of Supreme Court justices. Souter agreed with conservatives Chief Justice Rehnquist and Justice Antonin Scalia in 74 percent and 75 percent, respectively, of nonunanimous cases.[9] During Souter's second term, although evincing less consistent agreement with the most conservative justices, his interagreement rates indicate he was participating in, rather than clashing with, the Court's continued trend toward conservative decision making; he agreed with Rehnquist and Scalia in 65 percent and 67 percent, respectively, of nonunanimous cases.[10] Even in cases where Souter cast the decisive vote against the conservative justices' preferred outcome, Souter's vote was not a catalytic event. Souter's liberal votes frequently preserved the status quo, if only temporarily, rather than advancing a new decisional trend for the Court. For example, in voting to preserve the constitutional rule against sponsored prayer in public schools, Souter's vote helped to hold the line on a single issue rather than change the direction of Supreme Court decision making.[11] In other cases, Souter was endorsing a less than liberal decisional outcome that simply did not go far enough to satisfy his most conservative colleagues. In a controversial abortion case,[12] for example, Souter's vote upset the conservatives by preserving *Roe v. Wade*[13] as a precedent for providing women with choices about abortion. However, Souter's vote simultaneously approved a variety of state regulations that the original authors of *Roe* would never have accepted in that the regulations interfered with previously unrestrained abortion choices during the first two trimesters of pregnancy.

Thus Souter's appointment as a justice has given him the opportunity, in effect, to determine the outcomes in a variety of important, controversial cases. But because Souter's decisions, including those in controversial 5–4 cases, are generally consistent with the Rehnquist-era Court's conservative decisional trends, Souter cannot be regarded as a catalyst for significant developments affecting the Supreme Court's role and influence in American society.

Just as a single justice is unlikely to be a catalyst for political change, any single court decision is also unlikely to have a unique, longstanding impact on society. Individual case decisions have limited impact because they tend to be mere components within larger decisional trends that move constitutional doctrine in a particular direction. In addition, individual case decisions generally have no more than modest effects on society because the Court's efficacy in implementing any particular decision is vitiated by its relative weakness and inability to take practical enforcement steps beyond strong symbolic declarations. The Court must depend on other branches of government and the acquiescence of the citizenry for the effective implementation of its decisions.[14]

For example, arguably the Court's most famous decision was *Brown v. Board of Education*,[15] the case that ordered an end to government sponsored racial segregation in public schools. The *Brown* decision is generally credited with *causing* social change.

As characterized by one commentator, "Since neither Congress nor the states showed any inclination to promote civil rights, the Court's action [in *Brown*] may have been the only way to get the country moving on the road toward full racial equality."[16] Without denigrating the momentous symbolic importance of *Brown* as a courageous statement issued in the face of great hostility, there is reason to question whether the *Brown* decision, as a discrete event, should be viewed as the catalyst for the significant political changes that occurred in American society in the 1960s and thereafter. First, *Brown* can accurately be seen as but one decision, albeit an enormously important one, in a stream of decisions beginning in the 1930s[17] and continuing into the 1970s[18] that gradually led to the legal and practical elimination of the "separate but equal" doctrine underlying racial segregation. Second, empirical evidence indicates that very little actual desegregation occurred in the nation's public schools until the legislative and executive branches acted during the 1960s to provide inducements and sanctions that encouraged school districts to comply with the decade-old legal prohibition on racial segregation.[19] Thus even the Supreme Court's most famous and revered decision lacks the necessary attributes to qualify as a catalytic event that generated significant political change.

THE CONCEPT OF CRITICAL JUDICIAL NOMINATIONS

As indicated by the foregoing examples of Justice Souter and the Supreme Court's decision in *Brown v. Board of Education*, individuals and discrete events that apparently have immediate important impact (i.e., the appointment of Justice Souter) or are presumed to have caused social change (i.e., the *Brown* decision) cannot necessarily be classified as catalytic judicial phenomena that contribute to important social and political developments. If these apparent contributors to changes in politics and public policy are not actually catalysts for important societal developments, then what judicial phenomena can be classified as important catalytic events? To determine if catalytic judicial phenomena have occurred and are worthy of classification and analysis, there must be an attempt at conceptualization and definition of such important identifiable events.

A valuable method for identifying and developing useful analytical concepts for the understanding of the judicial branch is to consider borrowing and refining concepts and theories that have been applied to nonjudicial phenomena. One such concept of enormous importance (and subject to vigorous scholarly debate) for researchers who study elections and political parties has been V. O. Key's concept of the "critical election." In his seminal article, "A Theory of Critical Elections," Key identified presidential elections at various points in American history "in which the depth and intensity of electoral involvement are high, in which more or less profound readjustments occur in the relations of power within the community, and in which new and durable electoral groupings are formed."[20] These critical elections constituted moments at which the American political landscape was rearranged by the realignment of the electorate and the ascension of new governing coalitions.

For example, some scholars regard the elections of 1800, 1828, 1860, 1896, and 1932 as "fundamental turning points in the course of American electoral politics."[21] In 1800, the electorate shifted to favor the Jeffersonian Republicans over John Adams' Federalists. In 1828, the electorate realigned to favor the Jacksonian Democrats. Lincoln's Republicans controlled after 1860, and McKinley's 1896 election victory cemented Republican dominance until Franklin Roosevelt's New Deal coalition emerged to capture national politics in 1932. Scholars have subsequently debated whether Lyndon Johnson's landslide in 1964, Richard Nixon's election in 1968, and Ronald Reagan's electoral victory in 1980 should also be regarded as critical elections indicative of significant electoral shifts. Although political scientists continue to argue about whether the concepts of critical elections and realignments are accurate and useful for analyzing American political history,[22] as indicated by the flood of scholarly articles examining these concepts,[23] Key's original conceptualization of critical elections has provided a common language and focal point for scholars seeking to understand shifts in partisan preferences.

Key's critical election concept did not include every presidential election or even every election in which the White House changed hands. As defined by Key and as further refined by Burnham, the concept applied only to elections characterized by intense ideological conflict that resulted in durable transformations of the partisan alignments within the American polity.[24] The intensity and durability criteria in the critical election concept serve as indicators for the quality of importance in influencing political developments that a presidential election must evince in order to be classified as a critical election. Any judicial analogy to the critical election concept would also need its own set of indicators of importance. Such indicators are precisely what is missing from the previously discussed examples of Justice Souter and the *Brown* case which, while apparently contributing to political change, lacked the quality of fundamentally causing subsequent societal developments.

Borrowing Key's concept, it is contended in this book that there is an analogous concept applicable to the Supreme Court which focuses upon the two elements missing from institution-based analyses of the Supreme Court's long-term impact on the American society—discrete events and catalytic influences. By examining Supreme Court nominations, specific nominations emerge—here labeled as "critical judicial nominations"—which constitute pivotal, catalytic events that contribute to important changes in politics and public policy.

It should be noted at the outset, however, that the critical judicial nomination concept is not intended to provide a direct parallel to Key's formulation of critical elections. Presidential elections, especially those that mark moments of electoral realignment, are significantly more important than any judicial nomination to the Supreme Court. Durable changes within the electorate affecting partisan affiliations and policy preferences can reshape, sometimes relatively quickly, authoritative decision making throughout the entire political governing system. By contrast, because the Supreme Court is merely one component of the political governing system that must interact with other institutions and actors in order to be effective, the Court's influence on societal developments is necessarily more modest than that of critical elections. The underlying reason for borrowing from Key's concept is not to argue that events concerning the Supreme Court are as important and influential as presidential elections. Instead, the idea is to emulate Key in identifying specific events, in this instance Supreme Court nominations rather than presidential elections, that are associated with significant political developments.

Although the critical judicial nomination concept draws from Key's formulation of critical elections, there is a significant difference in a fundamental aspect of each concept. Unlike critical elections, which are frequently regarded as mere marking points for (rather than fundamental causes of) significant political changes, critical judicial nominations have a different role. Critical judicial nominations are catalytic events that *cause* consequent political and social developments and do not merely mark a moment in time at which political change is subsequently evident. Although critical judicial nominations are not the sole cause of political changes, they are important catalysts that arguably constitute a *sine qua non* for subsequent developments.

Given the important definitional distinctions between "critical elections" and "critical judicial nominations," how should such nominations be defined? *Critical judicial nominations are nominations that serve as catalytic events for important changes in politics and public policy that were not anticipated by the political actors who initiated the nominations.* Because this is an attempt at conceptual definition, the elements of the defined concept deserve further explanation:

1. The focus of the definition is on Supreme Court nominations rather than confirmed appointments because even unsuccessful nominations may generate important developments that alter aspects of the political system. The prime example of a critical unsuccessful nomination was President Lyndon Johnson's 1968 effort to promote his close confidant Abe Fortas from associate

justice to chief justice. The repercussions of that unsuccessful nomination significantly reshaped the Supreme Court and its role in American society during the 1970s. The focus of discussion for this book will be on Supreme Court nominations. Nominations for the high court normally generate the greatest political interest and impact of any judicial nominations. The definition of critical judicial nominations does not preclude the possibility, however unlikely, that a judicial nomination for another court (e.g., federal circuit court of appeals) might be a catalyst for important political developments.

2. As catalytic events, these nominations must arguably be essential catalysts for important political developments rather than merely minor contributing events amid concurrent larger and inevitable social trends that change American society. In order to be classified as critical judicial nominations, the nominations must be essential triggering events for the important political developments that follow.

3. The important changes in politics and public policy resulting from nominations identified as critical must be more than changes in specific case decisions. In order for a Supreme Court nomination to be critical, it must generate consequences for the political system that extend beyond the development of individual doctrines and precedents by the Supreme Court. Important changes, under this definition, must affect how the Court is viewed in society, how the Court interacts with other actors in the political system, or how other political actors, such as voters, behave in activities not directed at the Court.

4. Presidential motives in nominating new justices must be examined in order to understand why critical judicial nominations are only those which produce consequences not anticipated by the political actors who initiated the nominations. Presidents have specific political purposes in mind when they nominate an individual to become a Supreme Court justice. Generally, presidents seek to nominate someone whose political ideology and policy preferences comport with theirs. In nominating new justices, presidents also seek to please political constituencies (through the demo-

graphic or political characteristics of the nominee). For example, Ronald Reagan's campaign pledge to nominate a woman justice, and his subsequent 1981 nomination of Sandra Day O'Connor, stemmed from an effort to attract the support of female voters. Richard Nixon's unsuccessful nominations of Clement Haynsworth in 1969 and G. Harrold Carswell in 1970, and his successful appointment of Lewis Powell in 1971, were components of his efforts to attract the support of southern voters.

When viewed through the broad lens of all events and strategies occurring within the political system at a given moment, presidential goals and expectations for any specific Supreme Court nomination are relatively modest. Presidents may wish to see certain precedents overturned or judicial policies initiated, but they recognize that they cannot control what their nominees do after the nominee's confirmation. History has taught contemporary presidents that justices may be more liberal (e.g., Justice William Brennan appointed by Republican President Dwight Eisenhower in 1956) or more conservative (e.g., Justice Byron White appointed by Democratic President John F. Kennedy in 1962) than their appointing presidents could have predicted. With respect to nomination decisions calculated to generate electoral support, no president can reasonably expect to gain a significant favorable transformation among a sector of the electorate just by making one particular Supreme Court nomination. Thus, because of the relatively limited and specific nature of presidential purposes underlying nomination decisions, the fulfillment of presidential intentions by a particular nomination would not cause important changes in politics and policy. It is actually the unanticipated consequences of specific nominations that cause major political changes and therefore make those nominations "critical" under the definition. For example, as discussed in Chapter 5 with respect to the nomination of Justice Clarence Thomas, President Bush could never have anticipated that a nomination intended to advance specific conservative policy preferences and to attract minority voters would mobilize larger segments of the electorate against

Republican candidates and in support of liberal Democratic candidates.

The discussions of critical judicial nominations in the chapters that follow do not purport to provide a comprehensive theory about judicial nominations that would have predictive abilities for anticipating the consequences of future nominations. The concept of critical judicial nominations provides an alternative approach for analyzing the role and impact of the Supreme Court in the political governing system. Hopefully, the concept helps to illuminate aspects of the Court's influence and importance for American society that are obscured or omitted by analyses that focus on the Court as an institution or on the Court's decision making alone. Future development of the concept may provide useful refinements for defining and identifying critical judicial nominations and their conditional prerequisites. Further research is needed if any theory of critical judicial nominations is to be developed, defined, and evaluated. This initial effort has modest aspirations rather than grand pretensions in presenting a new concept and alternative approach for analyzing important events in the Supreme Court's history.

The chapters that follow will illustrate the critical nomination concept primarily through an examination of the 1991 nomination of Justice Clarence Thomas. Chapter 2 will discuss three critical nominations to illuminate various potential applications of the concept. Justice Thomas's nomination and impact on the Supreme Court will be analyzed in Chapter 3. Chapters 4 and 5 will discuss the catalytic elements of the Thomas nomination process and their significant consequences for the political system, especially with respect to electoral politics, before the concluding chapter assesses the utility of the critical judicial nomination concept.

NOTES

1. Dean Jaros and Robert Roper, "The U.S. Supreme Court: Myth, Diffuse Support, Specific Support, and Legitimacy," *American Politics Quarterly* 8 (1980): 85–105.

2. For example, Archibald Cox, *The Court and the Constitution* (Boston: Houghton Mifflin, 1987).

3. For example, one important study that calls into question the Supreme Court's presumed influence over significant social change is Gerald Rosenberg's *The Hollow Hope* (Chicago: University of Chicago Press, 1991).

4. Lawrence Baum, *The Supreme Court*, 4th ed. (Washington, D.C.: Congressional Quarterly Press, 1992), 19–25.

5. Walter Dean Burnham, "Critical Realignment: Dead or Alive?," in *The End of Realignment?: Interpreting American Electoral Eras*, ed. Byron E. Shafer (Madison, Wis.: University of Wisconsin Press, 1991), 124.

6. For example, Robert A. Dahl, "Decision-Making in a Democracy: The Supreme Court as a National Policy-Maker," *Journal of Public Law* 6 (1957): 279–95.

7. Christopher E. Smith and Scott P. Johnson, "Newcomer on the High Court: Justice Souter and the Supreme Court's 1990 Term," *South Dakota Law Review* 37 (1992): 39–43.

8. Linda Greenhouse, "Souter: Unlikely Anchor at Court's Center," *N.Y. Times*, 3 July 1992, A1.

9. Scott P. Johnson and Christopher E. Smith, "David Souter's First Term on the Supreme Court: The Impact of a New Justice," *Judicature* 75 (1992): 239.

10. Christopher E. Smith and Scott P. Johnson, "Justice Clarence Thomas: A Preliminary Assessment," paper presented at the annual meeting of the American Political Science Association, Chicago, Illinois, September 1992.

11. Lee v. Weisman, 112 S. Ct. 2649 (1992).

12. Planned Parenthood v. Casey, 112 S. Ct. 2791 (1992).

13. Roe v. Wade, 410 U.S. 113 (1973).

14. Charles A. Johnson and Bradley C. Canon, *Judicial Policies: Implementation and Impact* (Washington, D.C.: Congressional Quarterly Press, 1984), 29–184.

15. Brown v. Board of Education, 347 U.S. 483 (1954).

16. Melvin I. Urofsky, *A March of Liberty: A Constitutional History of the United States* (New York: Alfred A. Knopf, 1988), 773.

17. Missouri ex rel. Gaines v. Canada, 305 U.S. 337 (1938); Sipuel v. Board of Regents of the University of Oklahoma, 322 U.S. 631

(1948); Sweatt v. Painter, 339 U.S. 629 (1950); McLaurin v. Oklahoma State Regents, 339 U.S. 637 (1950).

18. Cooper v. Aaron, 358 U.S. 1 (1958); Griffin v. Prince Edward County School Board, 377 U.S. 218 (1964); Green v. County School Board of New Kent County, 391 U.S. 430 (1968); Alexander v. Holmes County Board of Education, 396 U.S. 19 (1969); Swann v. Charlotte-Mecklenburg Board of Education, 402 U.S. 1 (1971); Keyes v. School District No. 1, Denver 413 U.S. 921 (1973).

19. Rosenberg, *The Hollow Hope*, 42–54, 72–106.

20. V. O. Key, Jr., "A Theory of Critical Elections," *Journal of Politics* 17 (1955): 4.

21. Walter Dean Burnham, *Critical Elections and the Mainsprings of American Politics* (New York: W. W. Norton, 1970), 1.

22. For example, Everett Carll Ladd, "Like Waiting for Godot: The Uselessness of 'Realignment' for Understanding Change in Contemporary American Politics," in *The End of Realignment?: Interpreting American Electoral Eras*, ed. Byron E. Shafer (Madison, Wis.: University of Wisconsin Press, 1991), 3–36.

23. One bibliography of scholarly works on realignment contains approximately 500 entries. Harold F. Bass, Jr., "Background to Debate: A Reader's Guide and Bibliography," in *The End of Realignment?: Interpreting American Electoral Eras*, ed. Byron E. Shafer (Madison, Wis.: University of Wisconsin Press, 1991), 141–78.

24. Burnham, *Critical Elections*, 6–10.

2

Critical Judicial Nominations
in American History

A survey of Supreme Court history would reveal that relatively few judicial nominations meet the criteria for classification as "critical" nominations which significantly affected politics and policy. The three chief justice nominations discussed in this chapter—those of John Marshall in 1801, Earl Warren in 1953, and Abe Fortas in 1968—as well as the 1991 associate justice nomination of Clarence Thomas to be discussed in the chapters that follow, arguably provide the clearest examples of critical judicial nominations that shaped the Supreme Court's role or significantly affected other aspects of politics and policy in American society. The examples presented in this chapter are illustrative in the sense that they do not necessarily constitute an exhaustive list of critical judicial nominations that meet the stated definition. Just as V. O. Key's initial article on critical elections discussed only a few elections and left it to other scholars to refine and further apply his concept,[1] future analyses may find the concept of critical judicial nominations to be applicable to other selected nominations.

THE IMPACT OF JOHN MARSHALL'S
NOMINATION IN 1801

At the time that John Marshall was nominated by lameduck President John Adams to become chief justice, the Supreme Court was not an esteemed institution. According to David O'Brien, "In its first decade (1790–1800), the Court had little business, frequent turnovers in personnel, no chambers or staff of its own, no fixed customs, and no clear institutional identity."[2] Because they had so few cases to decide, the justices met together for only two annual sessions that lasted no more than two or three weeks each. Much of the early justices' time was spent in burdensome "circuit riding": traveling through their individually assigned states to join lower court judges in hearing cases. Justices also resided in their home circuits and engaged in teaching, practicing law, and consulting.[3] As a result, according to O'Brien, "some justices felt little or no institutional allegiance."[4]

The Supreme Court's lack of institutional stature and power was cited by John Adams' first choice for chief justice, John Jay, as a reason that he declined to accept the nomination. According to Jay, he did not wish to become chief justice because he believed that the Supreme Court "would not obtain the energy, weight, and dignity which was essential to its affording due support to the national government, nor acquire . . . public confidence and respect."[5] Although this was the state of the highest court at the point at which John Marshall was nominated and appointed, over the course of his thirty-five-year career as Chief Justice, he effectively transformed the Supreme Court into an important institution in national government and politics.

John Marshall was a committed Federalist who served in the Virginia legislature, the House of Representatives, and in the Adams administration as Secretary of State. An avowed political opponent of Thomas Jefferson, Marshall's appointment to the Supreme Court was confirmed just a few weeks before Jefferson became President.[6]

It has been argued that John Marshall's purported greatness derives from the fact that he was on the Supreme Court in its formative years, implying perhaps that anyone who was on the Court at that time would have had as substantial an impact on the development of the judicial branch. In the words of Oliver Wendell Holmes, Marshall presided over "a strategic point in the campaign of history, and part of his greatness consists in his being *there*."[7] However, such assertions undervalue Marshall's contributions and obscure the importance of his critical judicial nomination.

Marshall's personal qualities enabled him to capture the support of his colleagues on the Supreme Court and pull them along into unanimous decisions that strengthened the Court's institutional voice and enhanced its legitimacy. His warm, informal manner endeared him to nearly everyone who worked with him.[8] In addition, Marshall was, in the words of G. Edward White, "unquestionably one of the great legal reasoners of his time: contemporaries regularly testified to his ability to march from premise to conclusion."[9] More importantly, Marshall gave enduring meaning to constitutional interpretation through the

> invocation of the supposedly timeless principles of the founding age. The irony was that the principles had very likely not been conceived of as timeless by those who articulated them; only in Marshall's recasting did they become illustrations of the wisdom of republican theorists.[10]

In Marshall's interpretive hands, the Constitutional Convention was not a meeting of legislators trying to reach the compromises necessary to make a second attempt at creating a workable government after the failure of the Articles of Confederation. The Framers' immediate concerns about forming a union between the states that would not disintegrate and reassuring the states that the national government's power would be very limited were transformed by Marshall retrospectively into the founding of a unified nation with adequate power for the national government to address arising issues. After Marshall, the Framers are esteemed as remarkably prescient visionaries who expounded timeless principles of government that could endure and adapt to a growing, changing, and increasingly complex society. As described by R. Kent Newmyer, "Marshall's vision of the 'spirit and true meaning of the Constitution,' tidied up the clutter of history."[11] According to Newmyer, "Union was hypostatized into Nation; the government of limited authority, so much a part of colonial and revolutionary constitutionalism became a government of sufficient power. The Constitution became the symbol of that Nation and the source of its vitality—a living, dynamic organism."[12] Would any individual as chief justice have succeeded so well in defining the most important judicial institution, strengthening the national government, and establishing the language, customs, and style of constitutional interpretation for the rest of American history? Not likely.

Marshall played a singularly important role in shaping the customs and decision-making processes of the highest court. According to O'Brien, "One of John Marshall's greatest legacies has been the Court's ongoing collegiality."[13] Marshall used his amiable personality and intellectual gifts to achieve his goal of producing unanimous decisions that would strengthen the Supreme Court. Because he believed that unanimous decisions would build the Court's prestige, he discouraged dissenting opinions and ended the Court's emulation of the British practice of having each judge express an opinion.[14] The tradition of collegiality on the Supreme Court has continued in many forms. This is not to say that the justices do not disagree with each other and, during some eras, dislike each other intensely. It simply means that institutional norms were established for discussing cases, assigning opinion-writing responsibilities, and seeking consensus whenever possible. These practices are based on a recognition, inherited from Marshall's example, that the Court's effectiveness depends on the maintenance of its image and legitimacy as a judicial institution. Such attributes of collegiality and institutional concern remain in evidence on the contemporary Supreme Court. During the 1991 term, these concerns were primary for the conservative Court in the surprising abortion decision which upheld the fundamental principle of a right to choice that had been established in *Roe v. Wade*.[15] Justices O'Connor, Kennedy, and Souter issued a joint opinion expressing concern about the need to maintain the Court's legitimacy as a source of stability for society. According to their opinion:

The Court must take care to speak and act in ways that allow people to accept its decisions on the terms the Court claims for them, as grounded truly in principle, not as compromises with social and political pressures having, as such, no bearing on the principled choices that the Court is obligated to make. Thus, the Court's legitimacy depends on making principled decisions under circumstances in which their principled character is sufficiently plausible to be accepted by the Nation.[16]

Marshall's legacy endures from the major opinions that he authored which served to define and fortify the national governing institutions established by the Constitution. *Marbury v. Madison*,[17] a seemingly minor case about a disappointed officeseeker, thrust Marshall's Supreme Court into a confrontation with the Jefferson administration. Marbury had been appointed by President John Adams to become a justice of the peace. The appointment was made in the last hours of the Adams administration, prior to Thomas Jefferson and his supporters taking control of the executive branch. Marbury's commission was signed and sealed, but never delivered. Ironically, Adams's secretary of state who failed to deliver the commission was none other than John Marshall. Marbury followed the procedures spelled out in the Judiciary Act of 1789 by asking the Supreme Court for a writ of mandamus, essentially a judicial order instructing Thomas Jefferson and his secretary of state, James Madison, to deliver Marbury's commission. Marshall faced a serious problem because the relationships between the branches of government under the young Constitution were not clearly defined; it was not clear that the judicial branch could order the executive branch to take a specific action. Moreover, even if Marshall decided that the judiciary had the power to issue an order to the President, it was clear that there was virtually nothing to stop Jefferson and Madison from ignoring such an order. The Supreme Court had no ability to force the President to deliver the commission.

Marshall's opinion for the unanimous Court in the *Marbury* case is regarded as a tactically brilliant achievement that succeeded in asserting and strengthening the power of the judicial branch without risking presidential reactions that would have revealed the practical weaknesses of judicial power. In his opinion, Marshall asserted that the Court did, indeed, have the power to issue an order to the President. He also asserted that Marbury was entitled to his commission. However, Marshall declined to order Jefferson to deliver the commission because he found that the legal action initiated by Marbury under the Judiciary Act, namely seeking a writ of mandamus from the Supreme Court, violated the Constitution. The Constitution delineated the Supreme Court's original jurisdiction as "all Cases affecting Ambassadors, other public Ministers and Consuls, and those in which a State Shall be a Party."[18] The opinion stated that Congress, in effect, attempted to amend the Constitution by statute (i.e., the Judiciary Act)—rather than through the mandated amendment process—when it declared that actions for writs of mandamus were part of the Court's original jurisdiction and could be filed directly in the Supreme Court.

In this important opinion, Marshall asserted that the judicial branch was co-equal with the other two branches of national government in the governing system's scheme of checks and balances. According to the *Marbury* decision, the Supreme Court can issue directives to the President and nullify acts of Congress as unconstitutional. The *Marbury* case is best known for establishing the concept of judicial review, the power to determine the constitutionality of actions by other branches of government. Judicial review was discussed by the authors of the Constitution and their contemporaries, but the power was not explicitly granted to the judiciary by the Constitution. Thus the propriety and scope of judicial review continue to be subject to scholarly debate.[19]

Without any elaborate discussion of the competing arguments, Marshall simply asserted that the Supreme Court possesses the power to review acts of the other branches of government. Marshall's broad rhetorical assertion and his narrow action in striking down the mandamus section of the Judiciary Act established the concept of judicial review as a legal reality for the American governing system. The power was not exercised by the Supreme Court again until 1857, but beginning in 1865 judicial review began to be applied periodically to declare acts of Congress unconstitutional. There was a great acceleration in the frequency of the judiciary's assertion of this power after 1953.[20]

At the time of Marshall's opinion in *Marbury*, there was great uncertainty about the power of the judiciary. As a result of Marshall's opinion, the strength of which was fortified by Marshall's knack for securing unanimous support from his fellow justices, the concept of judicial review and the stature of the Supreme Court as a co-equal branch became established and accepted as components of the American governing system. If not for Marshall's opinion and its subsequent general acceptance, the modern judiciary might never have gained such influence over public policy. Although contemporary observers may disagree about whether the expansion of judicial power has been beneficial or detrimental for American society, there is a general agreement that Marshall was instrumental in laying the foundation for the Supreme Court's influential authority, role, and decision-making processes.

Other opinions by Marshall also solidified the institutions of national government. In *McCulloch v. Maryland*,[21] Marshall's opinion for the Court rejected a state's attempts to tax an agency of the federal government, a national bank branch. Marshall not only used the case to assert the supremacy of the Constitution over state laws, he also helped to establish Congress's broad, flexible policymaking powers by giving meaning to the Necessary and Proper Clause of the Constitution. Since the *McCulloch* decision, it has been accepted that Congress's authority is not limited to the powers specifically listed in Article I of the Constitution. Thanks to Marshall's persuasive opinion and its subsequent acceptance, Congress also has the power to take any "necessary and proper" action related to their specified powers. Marshall helped to strengthen the federal government's supremacy over the states, and he moved the meaning of the Constitution away from a conception of limited government and toward an interpretation that enabled the national legislature to take actions it deemed necessary to address important policy issues.

In *Gibbons v. Ogden*,[22] Marshall enhanced the national government's power at the expense of the states by broadly defining interstate commerce, thereby giving Congress wide latitude and exclusive authority to act concerning many commercial matters. Marshall's interpretation helped to diminish the likelihood that the Constitution would disintegrate, as had the Articles of Confederation, through interstate disputes about commercial matters. Like his other opinions, the *Gibbons* opinion illustrated Marshall's gift for broad, persuasive legal interpretations that advanced his Federalist principles:

The brilliance—and the legerdemain—of Marshall's interpretations was the partisan gloss he was able to put on the principles he extracted. Nothing about the word "commerce" *compelled* navigation to be included within it, and certainly nothing in the language or structure in the Constitution necessitated that the sole agent regulating commerce be the federal government. It was doubtful, in fact, that the Framers had even thought about state-sponsored steamboats when they thought about commerce, since the steamboat had not yet been invented. *Gibbons* was just the sort of case—new developments in American civilization giving potentially new meaning to constitutional language—that made Marshall's interpretive solution so compelling. . . . [He showed] that constitutional language was to be "adapted to the various crises in human affairs,". . . . [23]

This flexible approach to interpretation, despite potential protestations to the contrary by contemporary originalist theorists, has been adopted, perpetuated, and utilized by subsequent liberal and conservative justices who have adjusted the Constitution's meaning to fit social changes and their own policy preferences.

Marshall's imprint on the nation can be found in many other opinions during the country's formative years. In *Cohens v. Virginia*,[24] for example, Marshall established the authority of the U.S. Supreme Court to review decisions of state courts, even as he upheld the state court's decision. Marshall was a prolific writer and the dominant justice during the first third of the nineteenth century; he authored 519 of the 1,215 Supreme Court opinions issued between 1801 and 1835.[25] His impact on American history came not from his mere presence on the Court as the country's institutions were being developed, but from his successful efforts to define and shape the judiciary's resources in a manner that would build the national government's institutions.

Marshall's nomination was a critical moment in American history. His appointment as chief justice of the United States was by no means a foregone conclusion. After President Adams had initially submitted the name of John Jay to fill the Court vacancy, his associates urged him to name several other leading figures as the new chief justice: Samuel Sitgreaves of Pennsylvania; Charles Pinckney of South Carolina; and Associate Justice William Paterson of New Jersey. With minimal consultation from his advisors, Adams rejected the political advice and pressure to appoint others, and instead nominated Marshall because he felt that Marshall was one person who could be trusted to advance Federalist principles.[26]

Were the consequences of Marshall's nomination thus planned and anticipated by President Adams, thereby placing the nomination beyond the bounds of the definition of "critical judicial elections"? No. No one could have predicted how strongly and cleverly Marshall would mold the Supreme Court and use its voice to define and fortify the national government. Adams was undoubtedly pleased with Marshall's performance. However, given the president's relatively limited purpose of appointing a chief justice who might counteract undesirable actions by the Jefferson administration, neither he nor anyone else could have predicted the deep and lasting impact Marshall would have on the nation's history. At the moment in history when Marshall became chief justice, the country's future was relatively fragile and uncertain. Memories of the failures of the Articles of Confederation still lingered. Britain still threatened and indeed fought the young nation in the War of 1812 during Marshall's tenure. Thus Adams could not have anticipated the lasting impact that his critical nomination of Marshall would have on American politics and government.

Scholars give Marshall credit for developing the legitimacy and authority of American judicial institutions. He also is cited as "the primary creator of [the] unique institutional role" of appellate judges: "Since Marshall the appellate judiciary in America has been consciously aloof from direct participation in politics [yet it is] an active and weighty political force."[27] In establishing the role of appellate judges and broadly defining the constitutional powers and supremacy of national governmental institutions, Marshall "assured that the Constitution would be sufficiently flexible to keep abreast of historical change. . . . [I]t evolved through judicial processes rather than[, as the Framers had planned,] by formal amendment."[28] Thus the development of many important elements of American government and politics that are taken for granted by contemporary citizens can be traced back to the critical judicial nomination of John Marshall.

THE IMPACT OF EARL WARREN'S NOMINATION IN 1953

There is no doubt that President Dwight Eisenhower never anticipated the consequences of his 1953 nomination of Earl Warren to be chief justice: "When Eisenhower was asked . . . if he had made any mistakes while he had been President, he replied: 'Yes, two, and they are both sitting on the Supreme Court.' 'Both' referred to [Eisenhower appointees Earl] Warren and [William] Brennan."[29] Warren had earned his political reputation as a tough prosecutor and, as Governor of California, he was an instigator of the shameful World War II era policy of incarcerating innocent Japanese-American families in concentration camps.[30] No one could have predicted that his nomination would provide the critical event that coalesced the Supreme Court into a powerful and almost revolutionary force for expanding the protection of individual rights and thereby creating new kinds of judicial limitations on the policies and practices of government.

After the death of Chief Justice Fred Vinson in 1953, President Eisenhower's decision to nominate Earl Warren to fill the vacancy was not based merely on a miscalculation about how Warren would decide cases; Eisenhower owed a political debt to Warren for delivering the support of the large California delegation at the 1952 Republican convention. In addition, Vice President Richard Nixon and other rival California Republicans wanted the popular Warren removed from California Republican politics.[31]

Warren joined a Supreme Court that already included such activist liberals as William O. Douglas and Hugo Black. Unlike John Marshall, Warren did not play a singular role in providing the ideas and reasoning that reshaped the Court's role and influence on politics. Instead, Warren provided the leadership that pulled together an often fractious Court and led it on an accelerated path of unprecedented judicial activism on behalf of individuals' rights. For example, when Vinson died, the Court was deeply split concerning the pending case of *Brown v. Board of Education* and reargument had been scheduled in the case. According to William O. Douglas, the Court was split 4–4 over the issue of outlawing racial segregation when Warren entered the discussions after the second oral argument:

Warren suggested that the cases be discussed informally and no vote be taken. He didn't want the Conference to split up into two opposed groups. Warren's approach to the problem and discussions in the Conference were conciliatory; not those of an advocate trying to convince recalcitrant judges. . . . [A] five-to-four decision was the last thing any of us wanted. [Such a split vote] would not be a decisive decision historically. It would make the issue a political football. . . . As the days passed, Warren's position immensely impressed [Felix] Frankfurter. The essence of Frankfurter's position seemed to be that if a practical politician like Warren. . . . thought we could overrule the 1896 opinion [endorsing segregation], why should a [former law] professor object?[32]

Eventually Warren succeeded in convincing all of the justices to join his historic and controversial opinion declaring that state-sponsored racial segregation violated the Constitution. The unanimous decision by the Court was assailed by critics and resisted for years by many school districts, but by speaking with one voice under Warren's leadership, the Court made a powerful statement on behalf of individual liberty. As discussed in Chapter 1, the

Brown decision did not, in and of itself, change society. It took actions during the 1960s by the legislative and executive branches in the next decade to make desegregation a reality. However, the *Brown* decision is but one among many examples in which Warren's leadership moved the Supreme Court into a new realm of decision making that changed the Court's role in the governing system, altered political values in American society, and mobilized political interests in new ways.

The Warren-led Supreme Court affected public policy concerning a variety of issues. The Court gave meaning to the Fourteenth Amendment's Equal Protection Clause in school desegregation cases and in cases concerning such issues as state bans on interracial marriages.[33] Under Warren, the Court also borrowed from and expanded John Marshall's tradition of broad, flexible interpretation of congressional commerce power to endorse federal statutes ostensibly regulating interstate commerce that were actually directed at eradicating discrimination by private individuals in such areas as employment and public accommodations.[34] The Court stopped avoiding confrontations with the politicians who manipulated the design of legislative districts in order to dilute the votes of political opponents, and began to require that all Americans' votes would count equally in equal sized districts.[35] In the area of criminal defendants' rights, the Court initiated a remarkable expansion of individual protections that curtailed policies and practices of law enforcement agencies. During the Warren era, the Court decided its famous cases concerning such issues as indigent defendants' right to counsel,[36] police officers' obligation to inform suspects of their rights,[37] and the exclusion of evidence seized by police during unreasonable searches and seizures.[38] In establishing the famous *Miranda* warnings, Warren drew from his experiences as a prosecutor to create a judicial rule designed to prevent police officers from coercing defendants into confessing.[39] The Warren era also witnessed the expansion of rights for speech and religion, especially for people expressing unpopular or unusual viewpoints. Thus the Supreme Court issued controversial opinions such as the decision precluding sponsored prayer in public schools.[40] The list of cases decided during the 1950s and 1960s that expanded the rights of individuals and simultaneously limited the authority of government is extensive and worthy of book-length treatment. Such was the trend of decisions triggered by Warren's nomination.

The foregoing discussion is not meant to imply that Warren always agreed with the liberal decisions of his colleagues or that the Court always sided with individuals. In cases concerning symbolic speech, for example, Warren opposed providing First Amendment protection for political expression embodied in burning draft cards[41] and American flags,[42] and during the 1950s the Court itself occasionally seemed to back away from challenging Congress's desire to trample the rights of individuals suspected of being Communists.[43] In addition, because there were other powerful liberal voices on the Supreme Court during his tenure, it can be argued that many of the same decisions would have been made even if Warren had never been appointed. Warren, however, was the leader who brought the Court together to shape its purpose and voice. Although he did not control the outcomes of cases as his predecessor John Marshall did, nor even agree with all of his colleagues' liberal decisions,[44] Warren was the dominant influence who, as if an engineer driving a locomotive, moved the Supreme Court along its dynamic track toward judicial expansion of the Bill of Rights.

Earl Warren's impact reshaped the Supreme Court's role and society's political reactions to the judicial branch. Doctrinally, the Warren-era Court nearly completed the nationalization of the Bill of Rights by applying almost all of its protections against infringements by state and local governments. Despite the Constitution's clear words that "*Congress* shall make no law" violating citizens' First Amendment rights to freedom of speech, press, and religion, earlier justices had interpreted the Fourteenth Amendment's Due Process Clause to apply these specific rights against interference by state and local governments as well as against national laws enacted by Congress. Under Warren, the Supreme Court accelerated this expansion by applying this broad interpretation of the Due

Process Clause to other amendments in the Bill of Rights. According to David Bodenhamer:

Chief Justice [Warren] and his liberal associates on the bench left an undeniable legacy. Never before had a group of judges championed so vigorously the rights of social outcasts—racial minorities, dissidents, the poor, and criminal defendants. Never before had the Court given such substantive meaning to the time-honored ethic of equal justice under law. No longer did the expression and application of rights depend so much on accidents of geography. In 1961 only eight of twenty-six provisions of the Bill of Rights restrained both federal and state governments; by 1969 [the year of Warren's retirement] only seven guarantees remained unincorporated in the Fourteenth Amendment, thus restricting the central government alone.[45]

These changes did not merely reorient constitutional doctrine, they generated a fundamental alteration in politics and public policy. State and local governments found themselves closely supervised by federal courts and their policies were subject to judicial challenge by people who believed that their individual rights were being violated. This development not only limited the discretionary actions of legislative and executive branches of government at all levels, it also constituted a judicialization of many aspects of implementing and administering government programs. The judiciary became much more involved in examining the details of government. New policies developed with the assistance of, although not necessarily solely on account of, judicial action. Moreover, lawyers became even more influential actors as government units fought regular court battles against challenges by newly assertive individuals and interest groups.

According to Archibald Cox, "constitutional adjudication during the Warren era became an instrument of reform."[46] Conservative judicial activists in the early twentieth century had merely blocked actions by the legislative and executive branches. By contrast, many judicial decisions of the 1950s and thereafter attempted to initiate public policies and social change.[47] When the courts, during and after the Warren era, appeared to have both the will and the power to challenge other branches of government, political interests—including the weak (e.g., racial minorities) and the powerful (e.g., businesses)—channeled their resources into litigation as a means to either change or preserve desired policies. The courts became viewed as an additional available forum for the political policy battles in American society.

Some observers regard these changes in American politics as positive developments because courts began to listen and respond to the claims of politically weak individuals and groups who were either excluded from participation in or unable to succeed in the legislative and executive political arenas which majoritarian and wealthy interests effectively dominate.[48] Other observers, who are more skeptical about the efficacy of judicial power, believe that the judicialization of politics and public policy may have raised false hopes for many groups and caused them to expend their limited resources on litigation which would have been better spent on legislative lobbying and grassroots organizing.[49] Still others have viewed the Warren legacy of judicial involvement in politics and public policy as improperly damaging the primacy of demo-cratically accountable elected officials for authoritative decision making.[50] As a result of these clashing viewpoints, the rhetoric and strategic battles between the post-Warren political parties have focused on both the proper role of the judiciary and the specific policy issues affected by judicial decisions. The Republicans have focused their political campaigns and their subsequent judicial nominations on undoing Warren-era decisions affecting such is-sues as criminal defendants' rights, school prayer, and school desegregation. Democrats, however, have generally sought to protect policy gains in those areas and have defended activist judges who expand the protections for individuals. In previous eras, political parties have battled over the propriety of judicial decisions. For example, Franklin Roosevelt clashed with the pre-1937 Supreme Court which obstructed his social welfare and economic regulation programs. However, unlike the earlier era in which partisan battles diminished when the Court became support-ive of Roosevelt, the Warren era constituted a fundamental and enduring recasting of debates about the Supreme Court's (and other courts') proper role in politics and public policy.

THE IMPACT OF ABE FORTAS'S UNSUCCESSFUL NOMINATION FOR CHIEF JUSTICE IN 1968

When Earl Warren made known to President Lyndon Johnson that he intended to retire from the Supreme Court, President Johnson decided to nominate his longtime friend and advisor Abe Fortas for elevation from associate justice to chief justice. Simultaneously, Johnson nominated a Texas crony, federal judge Homer Thornberry, to fill Fortas's seat as associate justice. These actions quickly revealed themselves to be terrible tactical errors, and after Senate Republicans made clear that the nominees would be blocked from confirmation, both Fortas and Thornberry withdrew their nominations. The significant impact of this critical judicial nomination stemmed from the fact that the political battles over the Fortas nomination eventually culminated in Fortas's resignation from the Supreme Court. Thus Republican President Nixon was able to appoint four Supreme Court justices during the 1970s—two for retirements during the 1970s *plus* the replacements for Warren and Fortas which, but for Johnson's tactical errors, would have been under appointive control of the more liberal Democratic president.

Abe Fortas was a highly respected lawyer who was a founding partner of one of the most prominent and powerful law firms in Washington, D.C. His relationship with Lyndon Johnson went back to Johnson's early days in Congress in the 1930s, and Fortas provided the key legal representation for the future president's disputed victory in the 1948 Texas senate race.[51] Fortas maintained a close relationship with Johnson and, despite the impropriety of such actions, continued to secretly act as a close advisor for President Johnson after his 1965 appointment to the Supreme Court. It was probably quite logical for Johnson to want his close advisor and friend to be the chief justice when Warren stepped down. However, Johnson's actions in putting forward Fortas's nomination for elevation to chief justice seemed to clash with the President's well-established reputation for having remarkable political instincts.

President Johnson made several mistakes that doomed the Fortas nomination and, ultimately, Fortas's career as a Supreme Court justice. In March 1968 Johnson had become a lameduck president by announcing, in the midst of an increasingly unpopular Vietnam War, that he would not seek reelection. Thus he lacked the political power to pressure senators to support his nomination of his two friends to important positions on the Supreme Court. Although Johnson was urged by his advisors to appoint a respected, moderate Republican to take Fortas's seat,[52] Johnson went ahead with his own plans and gave Republican senators an easy, obvious target in the nomination of Johnson's relatively undistinguished Texas pal, Thornberry. Thus Fortas's nomination, inherently controversial because of his participation in liberal Warren Court decisions, was saddled with a nominee-partner who would be difficult to defend as sufficiently accomplished to deserve appointment to the nation's highest court.

Further, the lameduck president overestimated the willingness and ability of his old friend the Senate Republican leader, Everett Dirksen of Illinois, to deliver crucial votes from Republican moderates.[53] Johnson also managed to antagonize powerful Democratic Senator Richard Russell of Georgia by permitting Attorney General Ramsey Clark to block the appointment of one of Russell's friends to a federal district court seat.[54] By putting forward controversial nominations at a moment of presidential weakness, and amid serious political miscalculations, Johnson permitted the Senate hearings on the Fortas nomination to become, in the words of one scholar, "The Trial of Earl Warren's Court."[55] During a crucial election year, the Republicans in the Senate had an irresistible opportunity to attack the civil liberties decisions and judicial activism of the Warren-era Supreme Court, of which Justice Fortas was a part.

Because the nomination placed Fortas under the public spot-
light, investigations into Fortas's activities had repercussions for
the Justice even after he and Thornberry had withdrawn their
doomed nominations and President Nixon had assumed office
following the 1968 election. Controversies erupted concerning
Fortas's acceptance of an unusually large sum of money to teach
a course at American University's law school and, even more
damaging, Fortas's acceptance of a lifetime retainer from a foundation formed by an indicted financier who was subsequently
imprisoned. Serious questions emerged about whether Fortas had
in any way intervened on behalf of his benefactor to obstruct the
investigation and prosecution of a criminal case. Fortas had received one check from the foundation, but the controversy led him
to return the check and rescind the agreement. Fortas was not the
only justice to have such arrangements; Justice William O. Douglas received money from a different foundation. However, Fortas's
revelations emerged at a moment of great political controversy
when he was under the public microscope and Johnson's Republican opponents could use him for partisan purposes during an
election year. According to one scholarly study, Fortas was guilty
of greed and stupidity rather than any criminal or ethical impropriety:

All the justice had ever done was to accept and then return a payment,
which constituted his agreement to and then cancellation of a long-term
consultation. If Fortas was guilty of anything, . . . it was of insensitivity
to the Caesar's-wife appearance demanded of a judge as opposed to his
old role of a Washington lawyer. Or, if one wanted to make a less
charitable charge, he was guilty of outright stupidity, combined with
some amount of greed, in agreeing to take the money. . . . [It was]
eminently clear that Fortas was not guilty of . . . involvement in the
financier's legal affairs. . . . [But] given the way politics and the press
work, that was what the charge became.[56]

The Nixon administration mounted a campaign in the news
media against Fortas and supplied information to Earl Warren with
the hope that the chief justice would pressure Fortas to resign

because Fortas's ethical problems were tarnishing the Court's image. Eventually Fortas resigned, in part because of his own tactical errors in not making full disclosures about all of his activities when the revelations first became public knowledge.[57]

In 1969, Nixon appointed Warren Burger, a conservative law and order appellate judge, to be Earl Warren's replacement as chief justice. After two unsuccessful efforts to appoint southerners to replace Associate Justice Fortas, Nixon appointed Burger's long-time friend, federal Circuit Judge Harry Blackmun, to replace Fortas in 1970. When Justices Hugo Black and John Harlan retired in 1971, Nixon replaced them with William Rehnquist and Lewis Powell in 1972. With the addition of Nixon's four conservative appointees, the composition of the Court quickly and significantly changed. Although Justice Blackmun gradually became more liberal in his decision making, he was initially a consistent conservative on the Court. Chief Justice Burger and Justice Rehnquist continued their strongly conservative judicial careers. Justice Powell earned a reputation as a moderate for his decisions on abortion and some other issues, but scholarly evaluations of his career indicate that he was primarily conservative in his decision making.[58]

The Supreme Court under Chief Justice Burger did not reverse prominent decisions established during the Warren era. During the 1970s, the Court made a number of controversial liberal decisions, such as establishing a right of choice for abortion in the 1973 *Roe v. Wade* decision and establishing various rights for prisoners.[59] Although they did not engage in wholesale reversals of Warren-era precedents, and even advanced civil liberties in some cases, the new Burger Court justices began to erode specific areas of rights, especially with respect to criminal justice. More importantly, they halted the development of several important judicial policy-making trends.

In *Milliken v. Bradley*,[60] for example, a five-member majority of the Court (the four Nixon appointees plus Justice Stewart), stopped the development of desegregation plans for major metropolitan areas. In this specific case, the justices rejected a lower court judge's order to involve Detroit and its suburbs in cross-district busing, a decision made by the lower court because of evidence that the State of Michigan had joined the Detroit School Board in perpetuating discriminatory policies that could not be remedied within the Detroit district alone. By preserving the sanctity of individual school districts within metropolitan areas, the justices ensured that affluent suburbanites would not have to participate in the process of remedying the disadvantages experienced by the poor, minority students in urban public school systems. If not for the unsuccessful critical nomination of Fortas, it seems likely that one more Democratic justice's vote on the Court in 1974 would have revolutionized American public education by the creation of metropolitan school systems that mixed all students, white and black, rich and poor, in the nation's largest cities. Although such a judicial decision would have led to an explosion of political opposition from affluent suburbanites, it is difficult to know how the policy issue would have ultimately developed. Many analysts would argue that such metropolitan plans would have been doomed to failure by resistance from suburban parents or by triggering a concerted effort to approve a constitutional amendment to ban busing. However, because metropolitan plans were successfully implemented in individual cities that had unified, county-wide school systems, it is not certain that the policy would have been doomed by political opposition in every instance.[61]

Whether or not the judicial policy would have successfully transformed schools and equalized educational opportunities between declining cities and affluent suburbs, it seems clear that the Burger Court was using its "voice" to alter the Supreme Court's role in delivering symbolic messages to the public. According to Laurence Tribe, the Court missed an opportunity to make a statement against discrimination and unequal educational opportunities:

Even if it would have had no impact on judicial *remedies*, a judicial proclamation that inner city ghettoization was constitutionally infirm might have avoided legitimating this nationwide travesty [of severe racial segregation in large cities]. Had the Court exerted the one thing it clearly can control—its right-declaration powers—to recognize the role of law and of state action in creating ghettoization, the Court could at least have created positive social and political tension, the sort of tension that makes kids grow up thinking something is wrong, instead of inevitable, about ghettoization. Black leaders could have relied on such a positive tension in 1984, a decade after *Milliken*, to stress, as Martin Luther King did in 1964 [a decade after *Brown*], how much had been promised and how little delivered.[62]

In effect, the Court's primary role shifted back toward the pre-Warren tradition of endorsing majoritarian decisions that may adversely and unfairly affect political minorities. The Warren-era legacy of judicialization of policy issues continued as individuals and interest groups used litigation to pursue or preserve their preferred policies. However, the Supreme Court's role in the judicial battlefield moved toward braking further expansion of individual rights and deferring more frequently to the decisions of elected officials.

In *San Antonio Independent School District v. Rodriguez*,[63] the same five-member majority dominated by Nixon appointees decided that state systems that provide unequal funding levels for public school districts do not violate the Equal Protection Clause. Moreover, the five justices declared that the Equal Protection Clause does not protect poor people against discrimination that victimizes them because of their socioeconomic status. In the specific case, the justices rejected a claim from poor, primarily Hispanic parents who believed their children were being unfairly victimized by a property tax funding system that produced nearly twice as much money per pupil for nearby districts populated with affluent, white families.

If not for the unsuccessful critical nomination of Fortas, it is likely that one more Democratic justice's vote in 1973 would have revolutionized education financing throughout the United States by equalizing funding for school districts. States would no longer have been able to use property tax systems that provide extra benefits for affluent communities. In the aftermath of the Burger Court's decision to halt judicial reform of education, funding disparities continued to grow. By 1988, the original $238 per pupil per year disparity for the districts involved in the 1973 Supreme Court case had grown to a whopping $1,300 per pupil per year. The disparities between other districts in Texas were as much as $8,400 per pupil per year.[64] The Supreme Court, in its post-Warren posture of reducing judicial involvement in policy issues, left it to other institutions of government to address these disparities that caused poor youngsters to suffer from especially significant educational disadvantages relative to children in affluent communities. Of course, leaving it to other branches of government primarily meant leaving it to the elected officials in the legislative and executive branches to solve problems that they created and perpetuated in the first place on behalf of their politically powerful middle-class and affluent constituents. Eventually, in the late 1980s, state supreme courts around the country began to order equalization of educational resources within their states. The U.S. Supreme Court declined to redress the problem for the nation through a judicial decision in 1973, so the Burger Court left it to other judges to begin the process on a state-by-state basis nearly twenty years later.[65] As illustrated by the education financing issue, the Burger Court that formed as a result of the Fortas critical judicial nomination effectively reshaped the Court's role. The majority of justices no longer felt responsible for righting the wrongs of society.

With respect to the critical judicial nomination concept, it is clear that the consequences of the Fortas affair were not anticipated by President Johnson, and that the resulting Nixon appointments caused changes in the Supreme Court during the Burger era. The debatable issue concerns whether the Supreme Court's role and impact for politics and public policy had changed significantly or whether the Court was simply making fewer liberal decisions. Because the Burger Court did not actively reverse many of the controversial Warren-era precedents, some scholars have wondered "whether the Burger Court was only a transition from the liberal activism of the Warren Court to the reactionary activism of the Rehnquist Court."[66] Whether or not it constituted a distinctive era or a mere transition, because the Burger-era represented such a break from the unique Warren-era, it can be argued that the Nixon appointments significantly changed the Court, its role, and its impact on society. David Adamany implies as much by declaring that "[a] continuing retreat on individual rights by the Rehnquist Court would affirm that the Warren Court was an anomaly in a long history of judicial indifference or hostility to disadvantaged."[67] Because the Fortas nomination fiasco produced the Nixon appointees who shaped the Burger Court, and because the Burger Court made important changes in the Supreme Court's role, the unsuccessful nomination of Abe Fortas for Chief Justice deserves classification as a critical judicial nomination.

This view is supported by other scholars who regard the Fortas nomination as a critical event:

The unsuccessful nominations of Associate Justice Abe Fortas to succeed Earl Warren as chief justice of the United States and Judge Homer Thornberry of the United States Court of Appeals to be associate justice marked a critical turning point in the history of the Supreme Court. . . . Conceivably, Fortas would have gone on to lead the Court in the liberal tradition of Warren throughout the Nixon, Ford, and Carter administrations and, indeed, would have served 14 years until his death in 1982.

. . . Well into the Nixon administration, and perhaps even longer, the "Fortas Court" would in all probability have contained a bloc of liberal-to-moderate justices delaying, if not preventing, the [C]ourt's gradual drift in a conservative direction.[68]

ILLUSTRATIVE EXAMPLES AND THE CRITICAL JUDICIAL NOMINATION CONCEPT

The three foregoing examples each raise particular questions about the definition and applicability of the critical judicial nomination concept. The significant impact of John Marshall's nomination on American politics and government is universally

6. Henry J. Abraham, *Justices and Presidents: A Political History of Appointments to the Supreme Court*, 2d ed. (New York: Oxford University Press, 1985), 81–82.

7. R. Kent Newmyer, *The Supreme Court under Marshall and Taney* (Arlington Heights, Ill.: Harlan Davidson, 1968), 21.

8. White, *The Marshall Court*, 372; Newmyer, *The Supreme Court*, 20.

9. White, *The Marshall Court*, 373.

10. Ibid., 375.

11. Newmyer, *The Supreme Court*, 55.

12. Ibid.

13. O'Brien, *Storm Center*, 142.

14. Ibid., 137–42.

15. Roe v. Wade, 410 U.S. 113 (1973).

16. Planned Parenthood v. Casey, 112 S. Ct. 2791, 2814 (1992).

17. Marbury v. Madison, 1 Cranch 137 (1803).

18. U.S. Constitution, Article III, Section 2.

19. For example, Christopher Wolfe, *The Rise of Modern Judicial Review* (New York: Basic Books, 1986).

20. Alpheus T. Mason and D. Grier Stephenson, *American Constitutional Law*, 8th ed. (Englewood Cliffs, N.J.: Prentice-Hall, 1987), 33.

21. McCulloch v. Maryland, 4 Wheat. 316 (1819).

22. Gibbons v. Ogden, 9 Wheat. 1 (1824).

23. White, *The Marshall Court*, 375.

24. Cohens v. Virginia, 6 Wheat. 264 (1821).

25. Abraham, *Justices and Presidents*, 83.

26. Ibid., 81.

27. G. Edward White, *The American Judicial Tradition*, rev. ed. (New York: Oxford University Press, 1988), 9.

28. Newmyer, *The Supreme Court*, 55.

29. Abraham, *Justices and Presidents*, 263.

30. Ibid., 255.

31. Ibid., 252–53.

32. William O. Douglas, *The Court Years, 1939–1975* (New York: Random House, 1980), 114–15.

33. Loving v. Virginia, 388 U.S. 1 (1967).

34. For example, Katzenbach v. McClung, 379 U.S. 294 (1964).

35. Baker v. Carr, 369 U.S. 186 (1962).

36. Gideon v. Wainwright, 372 U.S. 335 (1963).

37. Miranda v. Arizona, 384 U.S. 436 (1966).

38. Mapp v. Ohio, 367 U.S. 643 (1961).

39. Christopher E. Smith, "Police Professionalism and the Rights of Criminal Defendants," *Criminal Law Bulletin* 26 (1990): 161.

40. Engel v. Vitale, 370 U.S. 421 (1962).

41. United States v. O'Brien, 391 U.S. 367 (1968).

42. Street v. New York, 394 U.S. 576 (1969).

43. Barenblatt v. United States, 360 U.S. 109 (1959).

44. For example, Robert J. Steamer, *Chief Justice: Leadership and the Supreme Court* (Columbia, S.C.: University of South Carolina Press, 1986), 68.

45. David J. Bodenhamer, *Fair Trial: Rights of the Accused in American History* (New York: Oxford University Press, 1992), 128.

46. Archibald Cox, *The Court and the Constitution* (Boston: Houghton Mifflin, 1987), 182.

47. Ibid.

48. For example, Lucius J. Barker and Jesse J. McCorry, *Black Americans and the Political System* (Cambridge, Mass.: Winthrop, 1976), 171–77.

49. Gerald Rosenberg, *The Hollow Hope* (Chicago: University of Chicago Press, 1991), 336–43.

50. For example, Robert H. Bork, *The Tempting of America: The Political Seduction of Law* (New York: Simon & Schuster, 1990).

51. Laura Kalman, *Abe Fortas* (New Haven, Conn.: Yale University Press, 1990), 199–201.

52. Ibid., 328.

53. Abraham, *Justices and Presidents*, 286.

54. Ibid.

55. Bruce Allen Murphy, *Fortas: The Rise and Ruin of a Supreme Court Justice* (New York: William Morrow, 1988), 407.

56. Ibid., 568–69.

57. Ibid., 569–77.

58. Janet L. Blasecki, "Justice Lewis Powell: Swing Voter or Staunch Conservative," *Journal of Politics* 52 (1990): 530–47.

59. *See, e.g.*, Bounds v. Smith, 430 U.S. 817 (1977) (right of access to a law library); Hutto v. Finney, 437 U.S. 678 (1978) (no extended solitary confinement).

60. Milliken v. Bradley, 418 U.S. 717 (1974).

61. *See, e.g.*, Gary Orfield, *Must We Bus? Segregated Schools and National Policy* (Washington, D.C.: Brookings Institution, 1978), 411–13; "A Tale of Four Cities," *Time*, 17 September 1979, 76–78.

62. Laurence Tribe, "The Curvature of Constitutional Space: What Lawyers Can Learn from Modern Physics," *Harvard Law Review* 103 (1989): 30.

63. San Antonio Independent School District v. Rodriguez, 411 U.S. 1 (1973).

64. Christopher E. Smith, *Courts and the Poor* (Chicago: Nelson-Hall, 1991), 105–8.

65. For example, Christopher E. Smith, *Courts and Public Policy* (Chicago: Nelson-Hall, 1993), Chapter 5.

66. Herman Schwartz, "Introduction," in *The Burger Years*, ed. Herman Schwartz (New York: Penguin, 1988), xxv.

67. David Adamany, "The Supreme Court," in *The American Courts: A Critical Assessment*, eds. John B. Gates and Charles A. Johnson (Washington, D.C.: Congressional Quarterly Press, 1991), 18.

68. John Massaro, "LBJ and the Fortas Nomination for Chief Justice," *Political Science Quarterly* 97 (1982–83): 603–4.

3

Justice Thomas and the Supreme Court

When Justice Thurgood Marshall retired from the Supreme Court in 1991, the high court lost one of its leading champions of the rights of individuals. Marshall was a member of the Warren-era Court for only its final years, but he continued the Warren legacy of judicial activism for two decades after the Warren-era ended. Marshall retired reluctantly because he had not wanted a conservative Republican president to name his successor. Because of his failing health, however, he felt that he had no choice but to retire even though Republican President George Bush was in the White House.

President Bush nominated Clarence Thomas to fill the vacancy created by Justice Marshall's retirement. The remaining chapters of this book will focus on the Thomas nomination as a critical judicial nomination significantly affecting politics and public policy. The clearest and most significant impact of the Thomas nomination was on the mobilization of women voters who affected the development and outcomes of various races during the 1992 primary and general elections. Chapters 4 and 5 will discuss this phenomenon and its implications for American politics and government. Although it is not yet clear what Justice Thomas's long-term impact will be on Supreme Court decisions, it will be asserted in this chapter that even Thomas's first term provided indications that Justice Thomas had an important impact on the role of the Supreme Court in American politics. Ultimately, Thomas's behavior may change, or subsequent appointments may lessen his impact. However, his immediate importance as a new justice on the Supreme Court makes him an intriguing figure worthy of examination to see if his nomination affected the Supreme Court's role while simultaneously triggering the more obvious and important effects on electoral politics.

THE POLITICS OF A SUPREME COURT NOMINATION

All Supreme Court nominations are determined by the president's political calculations. It is not a decision based on any abstract conception of "merit." Even in the one instance in which a president was pressured by bipartisan lobbying to appoint the most respected appellate judge in the country, Republican President Herbert Hoover ultimately appointed Democratic New York State Court of Appeals Judge Benjamin Cardozo in 1932 because Hoover wanted to gain political favor with key members of the U.S. Senate.[1] When presidents determine who will be best as the next justice, best is defined by the president according to the nominee's professional qualifications and the political benefits for the president and his political party that will flow from the nomination. Frequently, the partisan considerations are of such paramount importance that the nominee's professional qualifications must meet only minimal standards of acceptability.

Although the political motivations underlying Supreme Court nomination decisions are seldom difficult to identify, presidents seek to maintain their own reputations and the myth of the apolitical judiciary by refusing to admit that politics affects nomination decisions. Presidents always say that they are nominating the most qualified candidate. When presidents make obvious moves to appeal to demographic constituencies, such as President Reagan's fulfillment of his campaign pledge by nominating the first female justice, Sandra Day O'Connor, the presidents still maintain that they are appointing the most qualified candidate. As in previous nominations, the nomination of Clarence Thomas was motivated by President Bush's political calculations and superficially masked by Bush's assertions that Thomas was the most qualified candidate to replace Justice Marshall.

At the time of his nomination, Thomas was only 43 years old, and thus he was one of the youngest Supreme Court nominees in modern times. His relatively youthful age appealed to Bush and other conservative Republicans because they were continuing the Reagan administration's strategy of appointing young, life-tenured judicial officers who could shape decisions in the federal courts for decades after the conservative presidents had left office.[2] As a Supreme Court justice, Thomas may influence decisions on the highest court well into the twenty-first century.

Thomas was educated at one of the nation's most prestigious law schools, Yale, but his youthfulness precluded the accumulation of experience comparable to that possessed by many older potential candidates. Thomas worked for a few years each as an assistant attorney general in Missouri, a corporate attorney for a chemical company (Monsanto), a legislative assistant to Sen. John Danforth, and the assistant secretary for Civil Rights in the Reagan administration's Department of Education. Thomas's most significant experience was the nine years he spent as Chairman of the Equal Employment Opportunity Commission (EEOC) before serving as a federal appellate judge for one year.[3] His relative inexperience affected his evaluation by the American Bar Association committee that rates judicial nominees according to three grades: highly qualified, qualified, and not qualified. The committee has usually given Supreme Court nominees unanimous highly qualified ratings, but after examining Thomas's qualifications, the committee gave him, in the words of two journalists, "what was arguably the worst rating ever given to a Supreme Court nominee"[4]: twelve committee members rated him as merely qualified, two rated him as not qualified, and one abstained. No committee members rated him as highly qualified. His limited judicial experience (one year) and the relative narrowness of his administrative position which concerned one specialized area of law (employment discrimination) raised obvious questions about how he could possibly be the most qualified person in the country to serve on the Supreme Court. Yet President Bush introduced Thomas at a news conference by saying that Thomas "fits my description as the best man [*sic*] at the right time. . . . [W]e looked at this list [of potential candidates] with an idea of really finding the best, and I think that's what we did."[5]

For Bush, Thomas was the best candidate for two specific reasons. First, Thomas had established a reputation as an outspoken political conservative. He battled civil rights organizations and liberal critics as he changed the enforcement priorities and strategies of the EEOC in a manner, according to critics, that diminished the agency's previously aggressive stance against discrimination. Thomas spent the Reagan years traveling around the country giving speeches that criticized liberal judicial decisions and policies, such as affirmative action, abortion rights, and bans on sponsored prayers in public schools.[6] Bush and his advisors could readily presume that Thomas would provide an additional consistent vote for conservative decisions on a Court which already contained a solid conservative majority. [7] By saying at the nomination press conference that "the main consideration, in addition to excellence in qualification, is this concept of interpreting the Constitution and not legislating from the Federal bench,"[8] President Bush used the familiar conservative code words for advocating a judicial counterattack against the Warren-era legacy of liberal judicial activism. Presumably Bush expected Thomas to participate in the conservative judicial activism favored by conservative members of the Rehnquist Court who were intent on aggressively rewriting constitutional precedents and altering established interpretations of statutes.[9]

Second, Thomas was an African-American. By nominating Thomas to replace Marshall, the Court's first and, at that time, only African-American justice, Bush could avoid political criticism for creating an all-white Supreme Court. The president could simultaneously attempt to show racial minority group members that

Republicans recognized their accomplishments and were support-ive of their aspirations. Moreover, Bush could put liberal Demo-cratic senators in the awkward position of opposing Thomas only if they wished to bear responsibility for blocking an African-Amer-ican from an otherwise all-white Court. Liberal Democratic sena-tors would also risk accusations of racism, even from some of their traditional supporters, if they questioned Thomas too critically during the confirmation hearings. Although Bush's political moti-vations were apparent, he pretended otherwise and even expressed the "hope that there would not be political considerations" in the Senate's evaluation of Thomas during the confirmation proceed-ings.[10]

Although the Thomas nomination was designed to deter aggres-sive opposition from Democrats, the Bush administration devel-oped specific strategies for ensuring a successful confirmation. For example, Thomas personally lobbied for endorsements from prominent African-Americans so that their support would dissuade Democratic senators from opposing Thomas.[11] The Bush admin-istration launched a media campaign to focus public attention on Thomas's impressive life story with its triumphs over poverty and racial discrimination in the segregated Georgia of the 1950s.[12] The media campaign was intended to deflect attention away from Thomas's relative inexperience and controversial record as a Reagan administration official. In addition, the Bush administra-tion advised Thomas on how to answer questions posed by sena-tors. During the confirmation hearings before the Senate Judiciary Committee, Thomas adopted the strategy of avoiding specific answers about his views. The same strategy had been successful for Justice David Souter's confirmation hearings the previous year.[13] However, Souter, a former New Hampshire Attorney Gen-eral and state supreme court judge, had never taken public posi-tions on controversial issues. By contrast, Thomas was forced to disassociate himself from a significant body of strident speeches and articles that he had presented as member of the Reagan administration. While Souter appeared to be a moderate person when he skillfully avoided providing precise answers to senators' queries about specific legal issues, Thomas risked the appearance of disingenuousness by disavowing his prior statements and denying that any firm personal beliefs motivated his inflammatory political speeches. Thomas's performance in responding to senators' questions was also less impressive than Souter's because Thomas obviously had a weaker command of the details of constitutional law cases.

Many of Thomas's statements during the hearings illuminated the strategic evasiveness that he consistently presented to the Committee. When questioned about a speech before a conservative group in which he had praised an article that advocated outlawing abortion, Thomas asserted that "his praise was merely a 'throw away line' designed to interest conservatives in using the principle of natural law to take a more expansive view of civil rights."[14] Thomas then shocked senators and the general public by claiming that he had never discussed the abortion issue with anyone, not even when he was a law student at the time that *Roe v. Wade*[15] had been decided in 1973.[16] It was difficult, if not impossible, for many people to believe that a lawyer active in public affairs who made speeches implicitly criticizing abortion had no views on American society's most enduring political controversy of the preceding eighteen years and had never even discussed the issue with anyone. As Sen. Herbert Kohl of Wisconsin said, "He told the committee that *Roe v. Wade* was one of the two most significant decisions handed down by the Supreme Court in the past 20 years, yet he also told the committee that he had never discussed that decision and had no views about it. Simply put, that is astonishing."[17] Had Thomas said that it is inappropriate for judicial nominees to discuss their views on pending issues or even that he had discussed the issue but did not have firm views about it, he would have been criticized by liberals but he would not have made himself appear to be so disingenuous. By carrying his strategy of evasion to such an extreme, he gave his opponents ammunition against him and raised questions about both his qualifications and his veracity.

Thomas used a twofold approach to reassure senators that he was not the activist conservative that he appeared to be in his speeches and writings. First, Thomas claimed that his thoughts and actions in his role as a judicial officer were different than those in his role as a public policy advocate. Thomas told the Committee:

When one becomes a judge, the role changes. . . . You are no longer making policy. . . . [R]ather than looking for policy positions, you strive for impartiality . . . You begin to walk away from the development of new policies. You have to rule on cases as an impartial judge. And I think that is the important message that I am trying to send to you; that, yes, my whole record is relevant, but remember that that was as a policy maker not as a judge.[18]

Because social science evidence and historical experience indicate that justices' decisions are shaped by their political values, policy preferences, and experiences,[19] it was difficult for Thomas to argue persuasively that his record was not an accurate indicator of how he would perform as a justice.

Second, Thomas tried to reassure the members of the Committee that he was compassionate and sensitive to the importance of protecting individuals' rights. For example, when asked by Sen. Paul Simon of Illinois whether he could understand a Jewish child's feeling of exclusion when sent out of a classroom every day while classmates recited a Christian prayer, Thomas replied:

[W]hen someone feels that he or she is excluded because of certain practices, such as those religious practices, I think we need to question whether or not government is involved. I think it is wrong. . . . My concern would be . . . that when we consider cases in a constitutional context that we understand the effects of government's perceived endorsement of one religion over another and that we take that into consideration when we analyze those cases.[20]

Thomas similarly emphasized his own experiences as a victim of racial prejudice to stress his empathic understanding of victimized individuals who seek the courts' protection against discrimination and oppression.

Although many observers expected Thomas to overcome senators' misgivings and receive endorsement from the Judiciary Committee and the full Senate, Thomas's performance during the confirmation hearings served to raise doubts about the desirability of his nomination. The Judiciary Committee deadlocked 7–7, a vote that normally could keep a lower court judicial candidate's nomination from being referred to the full Senate. However, a chairman of the Judiciary Committee would seldom wish to be accused of depriving the full Senate of the opportunity to vote on a Supreme Court nomination, so Thomas's nomination went to the Senate without the expected endorsement of the Judiciary Committee.[21] The Committee vote was primarily along partisan lines with the tie created by the defection of Democratic Sen. Dennis DeConcini of Arizona, who voted with the outnumbered Republicans to support President Bush's nominee.

As Chapter 4 will discuss in detail, the Thomas nomination subsequently became embroiled in a roaring controversy concerning allegations that Thomas had sexually harassed Anita Hill, an attorney who worked as his assistant at both the Department of Education and the Equal Employment Opportunity Commission. In the aftermath of additional hearings on these charges and wrenching political debates, Thomas's appointment was confirmed by the narrowest of margins, 52–48, with Vice-President Dan Quayle in attendance for the purpose of casting the deciding vote in the event of a tie.

JUSTICE THOMAS'S FIRST TERM ON THE SUPREME COURT

The decision-making processes of the Supreme Court are affected by the relationships between the justices. During several specific eras, bitter conflicts between justices disrupted their ability to function as the collegial judicial body that Chief Justice John Marshall had sought to establish. Justices need good working relationships in order to seek stable majorities for their opinions and thereby present coherent reasoning that provides stability and predictability in law. According to Lawrence Baum:

A Court in which conflicts are kept under control has an advantage in achieving consensus in decisions because members work easily with each other and are relatively willing to compromise. Such a Court also may function more efficiently, because good interpersonal relations speed the process of reaching decisions and solving internal problems.[22]

Justice Thomas entered this collegial environment under a cloud of suspicion. His performance in answering questions to the Judiciary Committee, especially his implausible evasiveness regarding *Roe v. Wade* and his evident lack of knowledge about other doctrinal areas, could not have been reassuring to anyone knowledgeable about constitutional law, including the justices of the Supreme Court. In addition, the controversy concerning the sexual harassment charges tended to divide the public into those who believed Thomas's denials and those who believed Hill's charges. The justices may have also been concerned. In fact, one newsmagazine reported that unnamed sources inside the Court heard that "two conservative justices who watched the hearings told their clerks that they thought Thomas lied to the Judiciary Committee."[23] Such a negative judgment, if true, could easily affect the justices' willingness to cooperate and align themselves with Thomas in deciding some cases.

Justice Thomas's potential credibility problems were exacerbated by his actions after the confirmation vote. Several justices were reported to be "miffed at Thomas's insistence that he be sworn in . . . the day after [Chief Justice] Rehnquist's wife was buried."[24] The justices were also reportedly upset that Thomas and the Bush administration threw a huge party at the White House for the swearing-in ceremony at a time when the Supreme Court's justices and personnel were mourning the death of Mrs. Rehnquist. In substituting for Chief Justice Rehnquist at the ceremony in which Thomas took the federal, rather than the judicial, oath of office, Justice Byron White "was a bit acerbic that day . . . [and] pointedly referr[ed] to the death of the wife of the [C]hief [J]ustice."[25] Thomas subsequently took the judicial oath from Chief Justice Rehnquist in a hastily organized private ceremony a week earlier than scheduled because Thomas and the Bush administration feared further harmful revelations about Thomas by the news media.[26]

In an apparent attempt to repair his public image, Justice Thomas took the unusual step of appearing in a *People* magazine cover story written by his wife about the allegedly unfair confirmation hearings. Although Court nominees appear on the covers of news-magazines during their confirmation proceedings, Supreme Court justices normally only serve voluntarily as cover stories for popular, nonnews magazines when they are discussing, for example, the history of the Bill of Rights[27] or their reflections on the Supreme Court.[28] Thomas's *People* magazine article, by contrast, appeared more suited to a politician running for elective office rather than a life-tenured Supreme Court justice who would traditionally remain aloof from pulp magazine articles tinged with overtones of partisan politics. In the article, Virginia Thomas described the confirmation hearings as "spiritual warfare. Good versus evil."[29] The article included a series of photographs of the couple, including a "candid" shot of them reading the Bible together. This opaque media ploy to gain public sympathy apparently did not win much sympathy among justices on the Supreme Court: "The *People* magazine piece, according to Court insiders, was greeted with abject horror in the chambers of many of the justices and it brought the Court down to a different level [than the mythical image that justices seek to maintain] as did the charges against Thomas."[30] Because Justice Thomas's behavior may have antagonized some of his colleagues before his arrival at the Supreme Court, he may have harmed his reputation and, consequently, his persuasiveness and influence in the collegial decision-making processes of the high court.

There was unusually keen public interest in the performance of Clarence Thomas as a Supreme Court justice because of the political controversies that swirled around his nomination and confirmation. Although most observers expected Thomas to become a dependable addition to the dominant conservative bloc of Reagan and Bush appointees, Thomas's assertions about his judicial open-mindedness during the confirmation hearings raised questions about whether his judicial performance would differ from his pre-appointment conservative policy positions. Based on Thomas's record during his first term, it appears that his judicial performance will generally comport with his pre-appointment conservative policy positions.

By examining the justices' voting alignments, scholars can discern the formation of *de facto* voting blocs among like-minded justices. When justices demonstrate patterns of agreement with colleagues on case outcomes, observers can assess an individual justice's role within the Court's ideological divisions (if such divisions exist). Table 3–1 illustrates Supreme Court voting alignments for the 1991 term by showing the percentage of cases in which each justice agreed with every other justice. As Table 3–1 indicates, Justice Thomas maintained high levels of agreement with the Court's most conservative justices (Rehnquist and Scalia) and moderate levels of agreement with the justices who, in previous terms, had been considered members of the Court's dominant conservative majority (Souter, White, Kennedy, and O'Connor). The Indices of Interagreement beneath Table 3–1 indicate the existence and strength of Court voting blocs. Because interagreement ratings of .70 and greater are generally considered high enough to identify the existence of a voting bloc, the indices indicate that Justice Thomas joined only one strong voting bloc (with Justices Scalia and Rehnquist) and three borderline voting blocs (adding Justices Souter and Kennedy to the core conservatives).

It is notable that Justice Thomas's highest level of agreement was with Justice Scalia. Thomas agreed with Scalia in nearly 79 percent of nonunanimous cases. This was the highest level of agreement between any two justices on the Court during the 1991 term. Although high agreement levels may merely indicate the existence of compatible judicial philosophies, such high rates of agreement might also provide evidence that a new justice's bewilderment at entering an unfamiliar institutional environment caused the newcomer to follow the lead of an experienced justice. Early

Table 3-1
Interagreement in Nonunanimous Decisions of the Supreme Court, 1991 Term (percent)

	SC	TH	RE	KE	SO	WH	OC	ST	BL
Scalia		78.9	73.6	68.4	66.7	59.6	59.6	26.3	21.0
Thomas	78.9		71.9	54.3	66.7	56.1	54.3	26.3	28.0
Rehnquist	73.6	71.9		70.1	64.9	59.6	57.8	24.5	33.3
Kennedy	68.4	54.3	70.1		77.1	70.1	66.7	50.8	49.1
Souter	66.7	66.7	64.9	77.1		68.4	61.4	56.1	50.8
White	59.6	56.1	59.6	70.1	68.4		50.8	56.1	47.3
O'Connor	59.6	54.3	57.8	66.7	61.4	50.8		47.3	49.1
Stevens	26.3	26.3	24.5	50.8	56.1	56.1	47.3		77.1
Blackmun	21.0	28.0	33.3	49.1	50.8	47.3	49.1	77.1	

Includes only 57 nonunanimous cases in which all nine justices participated.

The following cases were excluded because Court divisions on separate issues contained within each case produced the absence of a clear majority: Sochor v. Florida, 112 S. Ct. 2114 (1992); Planned Parenthood v. Casey, 112 S. Ct. 2791 (1992).

Indices of Interagreement:

Court mean	= .56
Sprague criterion	= .78
Scalia, Thomas, Rehnquist, Kennedy, Souter	= .69
Scalia, Thomas, Rehnquist, Kennedy	= .70
Scalia, Thomas, Rehnquist, Souter	= .70
Scalia, Thomas, Rehnquist	= .75
Kennedy, Souter, White	= .72
Kennedy, Souter, O'Connor	= .68
Kennedy, Souter, O'Connor, White	= .66

Source: Christopher E. Smith and Scott P. Johnson, "The First-Term Performance of Justice Clarence Thomas," Judicature 76 (1993): 174. Reprinted by permission of the American Judicature Society.

in the term, the national news media noted that Justices Scalia and Thomas cast identical votes in the first thirteen cases in which Thomas participated,[31] including a controversial case in which Justices Thomas and Scalia were the lone dissenters when Chief

Justice Rehnquist and the other six justices identified a constitutional violation in the beating of a prisoner by correctional officers.[32] Media speculation centered on indirect influence by Justice Scalia over Thomas through a former Scalia law clerk who clerked for Justice Thomas during the 1991 term.[33] As the term developed, however, it became apparent that Thomas was not manifesting first-term self-doubt or uncertainty by merely following Justice Scalia's lead. Thomas parted company with Scalia in cases concerning such issues as criminal defendants' rights,[34] state taxing powers,[35] worker safety regulations,[36] and the desegregation of state universities.[37]

Although Justice Thomas had a high level of agreement with Justice Scalia, it appeared to be based on a shared judicial philosophy rather than undue influence because it was not uniquely high when considered in light of voting patterns in previous terms. The 1991 Thomas-Scalia agreement level was matched by several similarly high agreement rates between justices during the previous term (e.g., Rehnquist-Scalia, 78.4; Kennedy-Rehnquist, 78.4; Kennedy-Souter, 83.0; Scalia-Souter, 75.3; O'Connor-Kennedy, 83.0; Marshall-Stevens, 78.4) and was well below Justice Souter's nearly 89 percent agreement rate with Justice O'Connor during Souter's freshman term.[38] Thus Thomas's voting pattern appeared to reflect the expression of his own conservatism, a conservatism that coincides consistently with the views of both Justices Scalia and Rehnquist.

Justice Thomas's dissenting opinions also provided evidence of his conservatism and his close alignment with Justices Scalia and Rehnquist, the two justices acknowledged to be the Court's most strident conservatives. Dissenting opinions present justices with the opportunity to make a clear expression of their views without any concerns for the compromise and consensus required for maintaining support for a majority opinion. Thomas authored seven dissenting opinions during his first term. Only one of those dissenting opinions was a solo dissent.[39] The case concerned a criminal offender who was convicted of murdering a woman after he escaped from prison. During the sentencing phase of his trial, the prosecutor presented evidence that the offender was a member of a white supremacist prisoner gang, the Aryan Brotherhood. The jury subsequently sentenced him to death for the murder. When his conviction was reviewed by the Supreme Court, eight justices found that the death sentence decision may have been improperly influenced by the irrelevant but inflammatory information about his gang affiliation. Both the offender and the murder victim were white so the information was not relevant to the consideration of aggravating factors, such as evil motive, that justify jurors' determinations about imposing capital punishment. Justice Thomas disagreed with the conclusion that the information was improper and thereby indicated his willingness to strike out on his own in expressing disagreement with the other justices.

It is notable that Justice Scalia joined in Thomas's other six dissents,[40] but Justice Rehnquist was the only other justice who joined any of Thomas's dissents. Rehnquist joined four of the seven dissents. Thus, Justice Thomas's clearest assertions of alternative viewpoints were not attractive to most of his colleagues— only to the two most conservative justices on the Court.

In his opinions, Justice Thomas appeared to be most like Justice Scalia in his willingness to criticize other justices while employing less diplomacy than most justices usually use in their opinions. Scalia is well-known for his strident opinions that roundly condemn his colleagues,[41] as well as for his penchant for interrupting other justices' questions during oral argument. According to one close observer of the Court, "some justices . . . find [Scalia's outspokenness] irritating."[42] In some opinions, Justice Thomas manifested Justice Scalia's combative style and risked irritating other justices. As one newsmagazine noted, "Thomas can write in language that brings to mind Scalia's let's-you-and-me-scrap tone."[43] For example, in one case in which Thomas and Scalia were lone dissenters against the majority's finding of a constitutional violation when corrections officials beat a prisoner, Justice Thomas wrote, with a touch of sarcasm, that "the Eighth Amendment is not . . . a National Code of Prison Regulation" as he criticized the majority for behaving as if the Constitution can cure all social ills.[44] In another dissent, Justice Thomas criticized the majority's construction of a statute defining the crime of extortion:

As serious as the Court's disregard for history is its disregard for well-established principles of statutory construction. . . . If the Court makes up this version of the crime [of extortion] today, who is to say what version it will make up tomorrow when confronted with the next perceived rascal?[45]

In a case concerning a speedy trial claim by a defendant who was arrested several years after he was indicted, Justice Thomas issued a biting criticism of his colleagues' methods of analysis: "So engrossed is the Court in applying the multifactor balancing test set forth in *Barker* that it loses sight of the nature and purpose of the speedy trial guarantee set forth in the Sixth Amendment."[46] In yet another opinion tinged with sarcasm, Thomas accused his colleagues of excessive judicial activism in a case protecting the rights of individuals who are acquitted of crimes by reason of insanity but then are incarcerated after their psychiatric problems have dissipated:

The Louisiana statutory scheme the Court strikes down today is not some quirky relic of a bygone era. . . . Invalidating this quite reasonable scheme is bad enough; even worse is the Court's failure to explain precisely what is wrong with it. . . . Removing sane insanity acquittees from mental institutions may make eminent sense as a policy matter, but the Due Process Clause does not require the States to conform to the policy preferences of federal judges.[47]

Because of his combative style, Justice Thomas may not be able to persuade other colleagues to endorse his views in order to gain the majority support necessary for controlling a decision. Thomas's tone and style are not unique; other justices have used stronger language in individual opinions. However, his consistent disregard for diplomacy may affect his influence with other justices.

Scholars assess the importance of a given justice's opinion-writing responsibilities by identifying whether a justice wrote majority opinions in the cases cited by articles and books as the most important during a specific term. In order to classify important cases, Thomas's opinions were examined by looking at two broad sources: *The New York Times's*[48] and *Congressional Quarterly's*[49] reviews of the 1991 Supreme Court term. As in a previous study of Justice Souter's first term,[50] the risk of underinclusiveness was reduced by regarding cases as important if they were included in either of the publications' lists. According to these combined sources, there were twenty-eight important cases. Even when important cases are broadly defined, Thomas's responsibilities had relatively little importance according to this indicator of impact. Justice Thomas's lone important opinion was a plurality opinion, joined only by Chief Justice Rehnquist and Justice Scalia, in a unanimous decision in which the other six justices declined to follow the conservative triumvirate's reasons for extending limitations on prisoners' ability to pursue claims in federal courts.[51] Thomas's other eight majority opinions included four in which the justices were unanimous on the outcome,[52] two 8–1 decisions,[53] one 7–2 decision,[54] and one 6–3 decision concerning labor relations.[55] Three of these cases concerned the potentially controversial area of criminal justice,[56] but only one of Justice Thomas's opinions in these cases even generated two dissenters, and thus these were not among the most divisive cases decided by the Court. Thomas's other opinions concerned bankruptcy and other statutory matters.

From the mixture of unremarkable issues and general consensus in the cases for which Justice Thomas authored the Court's opinion, and from the dearth of justices willing to join Thomas's dissents, it appears that Justice Thomas was not perceived as someone able to persuade other justices to join him when the Court was closely divided. Chief Justice Rehnquist, who assigns the responsibility for writing the Court's opinion when he is in the majority, apparently trusted Thomas to write majority opinions when the Court had a strong consensus. However, because Justice

Thomas was combative in his dissenting opinions, and perhaps lacked credibility with other justices, he was not given responsibility for drafting opinions when it was crucial to compromise, use diplomatic language, or otherwise persuade key colleagues not to defect to the dissenting side which, in close cases, might then become the majority.

JUSTICE THOMAS'S IMPACT ON THE SUPREME COURT

The most notable development at the Supreme Court during Justice Thomas's first term was the emergence of centrist justices who previously voted consistently with the conservatives. Unlike the 1990 term in which a six-member conservative bloc (Rehnquist, White, Scalia, Kennedy, O'Connor, and Souter) dominated the Court,[57] the 1991 term witnessed divisions among the Reagan and Bush appointees and the emergence of a centrist group of justices (Souter, White, Kennedy, and O'Connor), between the conservative (Rehnquist, Scalia, and Thomas) and liberal (Blackmun and Stevens) blocs on the Court. Although they joined together in key cases, the centrist justices did not vote together as an actual voting bloc. Instead, they controlled the outcomes of most cases by creating *ad hoc*, shifting majorities as they individually joined the consistent conservatives or liberals depending on the issue presented in each case.

Why did this centrist group emerge when Thomas arrived on the Court? It is possible that the mix of issues decided by the Court in any given term may differ from that in previous terms and thereby generate greater (or lesser) grounds for disagreement among justices who frequently supported the same outcomes during prior terms.[58] Thus, perhaps, the particular issues concerning criminal justice and other matters did not divide the justices ideologically in the same way that the previous term's issues split the Court between the five conservatives appointed or elevated by Presidents Reagan and Bush (plus Kennedy-appointee White) and the three moderate-to-liberal holdovers from the Burger Court-era (Black-mun, Stevens, and, in the previous term, Marshall).

There is, however, an alternative reason for the emergence of the centrists; a reason which obviously affected several important decisions: one or more justices have changed their views on issues. Just as Justice Harry Blackmun became more liberal in the years following his 1970 appointment by President Richard Nixon, some conservative justices on the 1991–92 Court may have changed their views. When, as in Blackmun's example, the change in a justice's voting patterns develops gradually over several terms, it appears that the justice's philosophy is undergoing evolutionary changes that may stem simply from seeing issues affecting American society from a new perspective. This new perspective may come from seeing problems in a new light when feeling the awesome responsibility of writing opinions for the nation's highest court. A gradual change may also stem from the influence of interactions with bright, persuasive colleagues who present compelling alternative viewpoints in discussions of cases and drafts of written opinions. During Thomas's first term, however, the change for at least one justice was sudden rather than gradual. Justice Anthony Kennedy dramatically altered his views, in particular, on the highly controversial issues of abortion and freedom of religion.[59] Kennedy's majority opinions during the 1991 term supporting abortion rights[60] and opposing prayers at public school graduation ceremonies[61] differed markedly from his previous positions on abortion and on separation of church and state.[62]

In 1989, Justice Kennedy had joined Chief Justice Rehnquist's plurality opinion in *Webster v. Reproductive Health Services*[63] that provided a scathing critique of the fundamental abortion rights precedent, *Roe v. Wade*, and that all but openly declared that *Roe* ought to be overturned as soon as possible. In 1992, however, Kennedy coauthored a joint majority opinion with Justices O'Connor and Souter that explicitly upheld a woman's right of choice for abortion and emphasized the need for the Court to maintain stability in the law affecting abortion rights.[64] With respect to freedom of religion, in 1989 Justice Kennedy authored a strident opinion, joined by Chief Justice Rehnquist and Justices Scalia and White, endorsing government support of religious holiday displays despite the apparent conflict with the First Amendment's Establishment Clause doctrine mandating separation of church and state.[65] Kennedy manifested significant insensitivity to the feelings of minority religious groups by asserting implicitly that majoritarian Christians were victimized when judges prevented them from enjoying government support for their religious practices:

I am quite certain that ["the reasonable person"] will take away a salient message from our holding in this case: the Supreme Court of the United States has concluded that the First Amendment creates classes of religions based on the relative numbers of adherents. Those religions enjoying the largest following must be consigned to the status of least-favored faiths so as to avoid any possible risk of offending members of minority religions.[66]

By contrast, in 1992 Justice Kennedy authored a controversial Establishment Clause opinion that evinced great sensitivity to the feelings of religious minorities by extending the principle of separation of church and state to ban religious prayers (i.e., benedictions) by clergy at public school graduations.[67] In both the abortion case and the graduation prayer case, Kennedy's sudden switch in favor of the liberal justices' preferred policy of expanded constitutional protections for individuals provided the crucial fifth vote to narrowly prevent reversals of important precedents by the activist conservatives Chief Justice Rehnquist, Justices Scalia and White—and their new ally Justice Thomas. Justice Kennedy's abrupt and unexpected switches confounded legal commentators who predicted, incorrectly as it turned out, that Thomas's vote would determine the outcomes in the abortion and prayer cases.[68]

Why did Justice Kennedy switch sides so suddenly and thereby contradict his previous clearly defined stances on abortion and freedom of religion? What was it about the 1991–92 term that made it different from prior terms? Although one cannot say with certainty why Kennedy changed his positions, the key factor that was different during the 1991 term was the presence of conservative Clarence Thomas in the place of liberal Thurgood Marshall. Because the joint opinion by Kennedy, Souter, and O'Connor in the abortion case emphasized the preservation of the Court's legitimacy and the maintenance of stability in law, it appears that the addition of a new strident conservative may have jarred the less doctrinaire conservatives into rethinking the impact of suddenly reversing established precedents. Justice Thomas may have been the catalyst for repelling some of the centrists away from the justices firmly entrenched in the conservative wing of the Court. This certainly provides a plausible explanation for the timing and nature of Justice Kennedy's sudden shift on two crucial issues.

In addition, there are other reasons that some justices, perhaps those in the new centrist bloc, might be disinclined to be allied with Thomas's decisions. For example, the justices may separate themselves from Thomas in subtle or even unconscious ways because of their annoyance at Thomas's insistence on an earlier swearing in ceremony, his embarrassing cover story in *People* magazine, and as Chapter 4 will discuss in greater detail, his demonstrably questionable veracity in the hearings on the sexual harassment allegations. Moreover, Justice Thomas's votes, especially in the abortion and prayer cases, seemed to contradict his testimony during the confirmation hearings. Thomas's confirmation hearing testimony before the Senate Judiciary Committee was premised on the theme that he had not thought deeply about and therefore had not prejudged controversial issues, including those which had been the subject of his public speeches while working within the Reagan administration.[69] His claim that, for example, he had never discussed the abortion issue underlying *Roe v. Wade* with anyone in the eighteen years after its pronouncement was greeted with deep skepticism by critics. Because Thomas was so explicitly assertive in the opinions that he wrote and implicitly assertive by endorsing strident language in the opinions that he joined, especially the ones authored by Justice Scalia, he did little to diminish this skepticism about his veracity during the confirmation process. For example, Justice Thomas joined Scalia's strident dissenting opinion concerning abortion in which Justice Scalia wrote:

The Imperial Judiciary lives. It is instructive to compare this Nietzschean vision of us unelected, life-tenured judges—leading a Volk ... whose very 'belief in themselves' is mystically bound up in their 'understanding' of [this] Court ... with the somewhat more modest role envisioned for these lawyers by the Founders.[70]

By endorsing such strong language so soon after claiming that he had not yet analyzed the issue, Thomas created doubts about his truthfulness in responding to senators' questions at the confirmation hearings.

Justice Thomas's vote in the prayer case also appeared to directly contradict his statements during the confirmation hearings. In front of the Judiciary Committee, Thomas said that it is wrong for government to convey the impression of endorsing particular religions and thereby make religious minority group members feel excluded.[71] Without even considering the controversial question of Thomas's veracity concerning Hill's sexual harassment charges, Thomas appears to have been disingenuous during the other portions of his confirmation hearing testimony. This conclusion is consistent with a journalistic investigation of the Thomas nomination which reported that Justice Thomas told others, in effect, that he would say whatever he needed to say in order to win confirmation—whether or not those statements accurately reflected his views.[72] This pervasive uneasiness about his honesty and trustworthiness may further encourage the centrist justices to disassociate themselves from Thomas and, by extension, from the strident conservatives with whom Thomas agrees.

In the short term, Justice Thomas's direct impact on case outcomes was diminished by his embrace of consistently conservative positions during a term in which a dominant middle emerged within the Court. During the 1990 term, newcomer Justice Souter had a notable impact on Supreme Court decisions by casting the decisive vote in many 5–4 decisions.[73] Moreover, Souter's decisive vote in eleven such cases affecting criminal justice,[74] freedom of expression,[75] abortion information for clinic patients,[76] labor relations,[77] and punitive sanctions in litigation[78] probably produced outcomes different than those that would have emerged if Justice Souter's predecessor, Justice William Brennan, had remained on the Court. Souter's impact continued during the 1991 term because he cast a decisive vote in thirteen of the fourteen 5–4 decisions.[79] By contrast, Justice Thomas had a limited impact because he was a member of the majority and thereby cast decisive votes in only four of the Court's fourteen 5–4 decisions. Because Thomas joined the Court's liberals in two of those cases which concerned, respectively, law enforcement excesses in a child pornography investigation[80] and a civil procedure issue,[81] Thomas apparently determined a new judicial outcome only in the two other 5–4 cases in which his liberal predecessor, Justice Marshall, would have voted differently. These cases concerned limitations on judicial review of prisoners' habeas corpus petitions[82] and the interpretation of a statute regulating firearms.[83] Although Justice Thomas's immediate impact as a decisive vote to determine case outcomes was quite limited, his influence in affecting other justices on the Court and, consequently, the Court's role may be more interesting and important.

In the longer term, if Justice Thomas's presence as a strident conservative pushes Justices Kennedy, O'Connor, and Souter into the Court's center for controversial cases, the Court's spate of conservative activist decisions that rewrite statutory interpretation and constitutional precedents may subside. The conservative justices, especially Justice Scalia, have made it very clear that they will not hesitate to overturn case precedents with which they disagree.[84] Justice Scalia has stated forthrightly that "I would think it a violation of my oath to adhere to what I consider a plainly unjustified intrusion upon the democratic process in order that the Court might save face."[85] By contrast, Justices Kennedy, Souter, and O'Connor made it very clear in the 1992 abortion case that they are quite concerned about the Court being able to, in Scalia's terminology, save face. Their joint opinion emphasized the need to protect the Court's image as a thoughtful, dependable legal institution that does not abruptly change precedents, even controversial ones, when people have come to depend on that precedent over the course of many years. The centrist justices expressed grave concern about "the cost of both profound and unnecessary damage to the Court's legitimacy, and to the Nation's commitment to the rule of law"[86] if they cooperated with the conservatives' strident efforts to abolish individuals' right of choice concerning abortion.

Because Justice Thomas's strong opinions and consistent voting pattern placed the conservative wing on the verge of controlling the Court, the three less ideological conservatives had to confront the consequences of their continued association with the strident conservatives. Moreover, Thomas's questionable veracity and inappropriate actions may have made them even less inclined to cooperate and agree with him in deciding cases. Thus the 1991 term may be a harbinger of a shift in the Court's behavior in which the centrist justices effectively control case outcomes to produce some liberal decisions amid generally conservative decisional trends as they attempt to keep the Court on a steady course.[87] The Court's pattern of decisions is likely to remain conservative overall because of the near monopoly of Republican justices, but doctrinal changes could be more incremental and established precedents might be preserved in whole or in part if the centrists dominate. As a result, the Court's role in the political system may become less intrusive and controversial as neither the activist conservatives nor the activist liberals control case outcomes. Although firm conclusions about the Court's direction and the consequences of changes in its role must await the analysis of decisions from additional Supreme Court terms, it appears that Justice Thomas's nomination may deserve classification as a critical judicial nomination if the centrist group coalesces and dominates the Court as a result.

NOTES

1. Henry J. Abraham, *Justices and Presidents: A Political History of Appointments to the Supreme Court*, 2d ed. (New York: Oxford University Press, 1985), 201–2.

2. Herman Schwartz, *Packing the Courts: The Conservative Campaign to Rewrite the Constitution* (New York: Charles Scribner's Sons, 1988), 90–94.

3. "Supreme Mystery," *Newsweek*, 16 September 1991, 18–31.

4. Timothy M. Phelps and Helen Winternitz, *Capitol Games* (New York: Hyperion, 1992), 140–41.

5. "Excerpts From News Conference Announcing Court Nominee," *N.Y. Times*, 2 July 1991, A10.

6. Evan Thomas, "Where Does He Stand?" *Newsweek*, 15 July 1991, 16–17.

7. For example, Scott P. Johnson and Christopher E. Smith, "David Souter's First Term on the Supreme Court: The Impact of a New Justice," *Judicature* 75 (1992): 238–43.

8. "Excerpts From News Conference," A10.

9. Christopher E. Smith, "The Supreme Court's Emerging Majority: Restraining the High Court or Transforming Its Role?" *Akron Law Review* 24 (1990): 393–421.

10. "Excerpts From News Conference," A10.

11. Gary Lee, "Running Hard for a Place On the Bench," *Washington Post National Weekly Edition*, 19–25 August 1991, 12.

12. "Liberals and the Lessons of Bork," *Newsweek*, 12 August 1991, 26.

13. Roe v. Wade, 410 U.S. 113 (1973).

14. Ruth Marcus, "Haven't We Met Before?: If You Liked the Souter Hearings, Then You Love the Thomas Replay," *Washington Post National Weekly Edition*, 23–29 September 1991, 14.

15. Linda Greenhouse, "Trying to Define Clarence Thomas," *N.Y. Times*, 15 September 1991, 17.

16. "Excerpts from Senate's Hearings on Thomas Nomination," *N.Y. Times*, 11 September 1991.

17. "Excerpts from Remarks by Members of Senate Judiciary Panel on Thomas," *N.Y. Times*, 28 September 1991, 8.

18. "Excerpts from Senate's Hearing on the Thomas Nomination," *N.Y. Times*, 13 September 1991, A18.

19. For example, C. Neal Tate and Roger Handberg, "Time Binding and Theory Building in Personal Attribute Models of Supreme Court Behavior, 1916–88," *American Journal of Political Science* 35 (1991): 460–80.

20. "Excerpts from Senate Hearings on the Thomas Nomination," *N.Y. Times*, 12 September 1991, A10.

21. Richard L. Berke, "After Panel's Tie Vote on Thomas, Maneuvering Shifts to the Senate Floor," *N.Y. Times*, 29 September 1991, A16.

22. Lawrence Baum, *The Supreme Court*, 4th ed. (Washington, D.C.: Congressional Quarterly Press, 1992), 166.

23. David A. Kaplan, "An Uncomfortable Seat," *Newsweek*, 28 October 1991, 31.

24. Karen O'Connor, "The Effects of the Thomas Appointment to the Supreme Court," *PS: Political Science & Politics* 25 (1992): 495.

25. Phelps and Winternitz, *Capitol Games*, xvi.

26. Ibid., xiii–xvii.

27. For example, Warren E. Burger, "The Bill of Rights: What It Means to Us," *Parade Magazine* 14 (January 1991): 4–6.

28. For example, Jeffrey T. Leeds, "A Life on the Court," *N.Y. Times Magazine*, 5 October 1986.

29. Virginia Lamp Thomas, "Breaking Silence," *People*, 11 November 1991, 108–16.

30. O'Connor, "The Effects of the Thomas Appointment," 495.

31. For example, "The Justices Scold Thomas," *Time*, 9 March 1992, 31.

32. Hudson v. McMillian, 112 S. Ct. 995 (1992).

33. "Thomas: Hypocritic Oath?" *Newsweek*, 9 March 1992, 6.

34. Dawson v. Delaware, 112 S. Ct. 1093 (1992); Keeney v. Tamayo-Reyes, 112 S. Ct. 1715 (1992); Georgia v. McCollum, 112 S.Ct. 2348 (1992).

35. Allied-Signal, Inc. v. Director, Division of Taxation, 112 S. Ct. 2251 (1992).

36. Gade v. National Solid Waste Management Association, 112 S. Ct. 2374 (1992).

37. United States v. Fordice, 112 S. Ct. 2727 (1992).

38. For example, Johnson and Smith, "David Souter's first term," 238–43.

39. Dawson v. Delaware, 112 S. Ct. 1093 (1992).

40. Wyoming v. Oklahoma, 112 S. Ct. 789 (1992); Hudson v. McMillian, 112 S. Ct. 995 (1992); Foucha v. Louisiana, 112 S. Ct. 1780 (1992); Riggins v. Nevada, 112 S. Ct. 1810 (1992); Evans v. United States, 112 S. Ct. 1881 (1992); Doggett v. United States, 112 S. Ct. 2686 (1992).

41. For example, Christopher E. Smith, "Justice Antonin Scalia and the Institutions of American Government," *Wake Forest Law Review* 25 (1990): 783, 805–8.

42. David M. O'Brien, *Storm Center: The Supreme Court in American Politics*, 2d ed. (New York: W. W. Norton, 1990), 274.

43. "Judging Thomas," *Time*, 13 July 1992, 30.

44. Hudson v. McMillian, 112 S. Ct. 995, 1010 (1992) (Thomas, J., dissenting).

45. Evans v. United States, 112 S. Ct. 1881, 1899, 1904 (1992) (Thomas, J., dissenting).

46. Doggett v. United States, 112 S. Ct 2686, 2700 (1992) (Thomas, J., dissenting).

47. Foucha v. Louisiana, 112 S. Ct. 1780, 1797, 1809 (1992) (Thomas, J., dissenting).

48. Linda Greenhouse, "Moderates on Court Defy Predictions," *N.Y. Times*, 5 July 1992.

49. "Highlights of Term," *Congressional Quarterly* 50 (1992): 1960.

50. Johnson and Smith, "David Souter's First Term," 242.

51. Wright v. West, 112 S. Ct. 2482 (1992).

52. The unanimous opinions came in Molzof v. United States, 112 S. Ct. 711 (1992); Holywell Corporation v. Smith, 112 S. Ct. 1021 (1992); and Robertson v. Seattle Audubon Society, 112 S. Ct. 1407 (1992). In Connecticut National Bank v. Germain, 112 S. Ct. 1021 (1992), there were four concurring justices.

53. Taylor v. Freeland and Kronz, 112 S. Ct. 1644 (1992); United States v. Salerno, 112 S. Ct. 2503 (1992).

54. United States v. Wilson, 112 S. Ct. 1351 (1992).

55. Lechmere v. National Labor Relations Board, 112 S. Ct. 841 (1992).

56. United States v. Wilson, 112 S. Ct. 1351 (1992); Wright v. West, 112 S. Ct. 2482 (1992); United States v. Salerno, 112 S.Ct. 2503 (1992).

57. Johnson and Smith, "David Souter's First Term," 239.

58. For example, Lawrence Baum, "Measuring Policy Change in the U.S. Supreme Court," *American Political Science Review* 82 (1988): 905–12.

59. For example, Richard Lacayo, "Inside the Court: Justice Kennedy Flipped Positions to Uphold Abortion Rights. Why Did He Change His Mind?," *Time*, 13 July 1992, 29.

60. Planned Parenthood v. Casey, 112 S. Ct. 2791 (1992).

61. Lee v. Weisman, 112 S. Ct. 2649 (1992).

62. For example, Christopher E. Smith, "Supreme Court Surprise: Justice Anthony Kennedy's Move Toward Moderation," *Oklahoma Law Review* 45 (1992): 459–76.

63. Webster v. Reproductive Health Services, 109 S. Ct. 3040 (1989).

64. Planned Parenthood v. Casey, 112 S. Ct. 2791 (1992).

65. County of Allegheny v. A.C.L.U., 109 S. Ct. 3086 (1989).

66. Ibid., 3145 (Kennedy, J., concurring in part and dissenting in part).

67. Lee v. Weisman, 112 S. Ct. 2649 (1992).

68. For example, Christopher E. Smith and Linda Fry, "Vigilance or Accommodation: The Changing Supreme Court and Religious Freedom," *Syracuse Law Review* 42 (1991): 893–944.

69. For example, Greenhouse, "Trying to Define Clarence Thomas," 17.

70. Planned Parenthood v. Casey, 112 S. Ct. 2791, 2882 (1992) (Scalia, J., dissenting).

71. "Excerpts From Senate Hearings on the Thomas Nomination," 12 September 1991, A10.

72. Phelps and Winternitz, *Capitol Games*, 178.

73. Christopher E. Smith and Scott P. Johnson, "Newcomer on the High Court: Justice Souter and the Supreme Court's 1990 Term," *South Dakota Law Review* 37 (1992): 21–43.

74. Arizona v. Fulminante, 111 S. Ct. 1246 (1991); County of Riverside v. McLaughlin, 111 S. Ct. 1661 (1991); Mu'min v. Virginia, 111 S. Ct. 1899 (1991); Wilson v. Seiter, 111 S. Ct. 2321 (1991); Schad v. Arizona, 111 S. Ct. 2491 (1991); Peretz v. United States, 111 S. Ct. 2661 (1991); Harmelin v. Michigan, 111 S. Ct. 2680 (1991).

75. Barnes v. Glen Theatre, Inc., 111 S. Ct. 2456 (1991).

76. Rust v. Sullivan, 111 S. Ct. 1759 (1991).

77. Litton Financial Printing Division v. National Labor Relations Board, 111 S. Ct. 2215 (1991).

78. Business Guides, Inc. v. Chromatic Communications Enterprises, Inc., 111 S. Ct. 922 (1991).

79. Linda Greenhouse, "Souter: Unlikely Anchor at Court's Center," *N.Y. Times*, 3 July 1992, A1.

80. Jacobson v. United States, 112 S. Ct. 1535 (1992).

81. American National Red Cross v. S.G., 112 S. Ct. 2465 (1992).

82. Keeney v. Tamayo-Reyes, 112 S. Ct. 1715 (1992).

83. United States v. Thompson/Center Arms Co., 112 S. Ct. 2102 (1992).

84. Christopher E. Smith, "The Supreme Court in Transition: Assessing the Legitimacy of the Leading Legal Institution," *Kentucky Law Journal* 79 (1990–91): 336–38.

85. South Carolina v. Gathers, 109 S. Ct. 2207, 2218 (1989) (Scalia, J., dissenting).

86. Planned Parenthood v. Casey, 112 S. Ct. 2791, 2816 (1992).

87. For example, Linda Greenhouse, "Changed Path for Court?: New Balance Is Held by 3 Cautious Justices," *N.Y. Times*, 26 June 1992.

4

The Thomas Hearings as the Catalyst for Political Mobilization

Unlike the three illustrative critical judicial nominations described in Chapter 2, which affected the Supreme Court's role and impact on politics, the Thomas nomination's impact leaped beyond the judicial branch to directly affect segments of the electorate and specific election campaigns. In October 1991, the nation's attention was captured by the spectacle of the Senate Judiciary Committee grappling with allegations of sexual harassment raised against a Supreme Court nominee by his former assistant. The senators purported to seek the truth about the allegations, but partisan interests governed their behavior in either attacking Anita Hill, challenging Clarence Thomas's denials, or, more commonly, evincing bewilderment about how to get through the controversy quickly without suffering excessive political damage in the eyes of constituents. The lingering image in the minds of many observers, especially educated female voters, was of fourteen middle-aged white males demonstrating convincingly their insensitivity and lack of understanding about sexual harassment as they permitted or, in some cases, planned and executed unfair, politically motivated attacks on the alleged discrimination victim. Thus although the mobilization of women voters occurred as a result of the critical Thomas nomination, it was triggered more by what the public learned about the Senate during the confirmation process than by what Thomas said during the hearings. In order to lay the groundwork for the discussion in Chapter 5 concerning the political consequences of the Thomas nomination, this chapter will discuss in detail aspects of the Judiciary Committee's hearings on the sexual harassment allegations that generated outrage in many female voters.

THE POLITICAL MOTIVATIONS UNDERLYING THE CONFIRMATION VOTE

During October of 1991, the American public witnessed on live television the unprecedented spectacle of a Supreme Court nominee facing accusations of sexual harassment. The rancorous hearings and ultimate confirmation of the alleged harasser, Clarence Thomas, left bitter feelings and deep scars among many segments of American society.[1] The search for truth in the Senate Judiciary Committee's Anita Hill-Clarence Thomas hearings was obscured by a limited time period for careful inquiry and analysis of information, partisan maneuvering, varying perceptions about the nature of sexual harassment, and the glare of television klieg lights.

Clarence Thomas became the focus of political battles when his nomination to replace retiring Justice Thurgood Marshall, one of the most liberal justices ever to sit on the Court, was perceived to solidify further the conservative justices' control over the Supreme Court. After the Senate Judiciary Committee questioned Thomas and deadlocked, 7–7, in voting on his nomination, Thomas's nomination process took a bizarre and controversial turn that, according to the press, "stunned the nation."[2] Thomas was forced to face the Judiciary Committee yet again, as well as a nationwide television audience, to answer charges by law professor Anita Hill that he had sexually harassed her when she was his assistant at the U.S. Department of Education and the Equal Employment Opportunity Commission eight years earlier.[3] Hill specifically alleged that Thomas not only made unwanted advances toward her, but that he also used graphic sexual terms in conversations with her and suggested that she should watch pornographic films.

As "modern history's nastiest Supreme Court confirmation fight,"[4] the Hill-Thomas hearings captured the nation's attention and raised significant questions about relationships between men and women, the status of women in American society, and the effectiveness and fairness of the Senate's confirmation process for Supreme Court nominees. Lurking beneath people's assessments of these overriding issues was the basic question: Who was telling the truth, Hill or Thomas?

Because the Senate hearings were *not* conducted as a truth-seeking process, it is obvious that Thomas's final 52–48 confirmation vote did not rest on a complete determination of the disputants' veracity. The senators' behavior during the Hill-Thomas controversy and their ultimate votes on Thomas's confirmation were guided primarily by political considerations. Based upon their political party affiliations, constituents' wishes, and policy preferences, most senators had made up their minds about Thomas's desirability as a Supreme Court justice after the first round of hearings and before Hill's allegations came to light.[5] Although some of Thomas's more tentative supporters publicly backed away, at least temporarily, until the Judiciary Committee could examine the harassment charges,[6] only three Democratic senators reversed their previously announced support for Thomas after Hill gave her testimony.[7] Ultimately, the "vote to confirm Judge Thomas was a search for safe political ground."[8] Legislators' decisions are generally governed by their own political self-preservation, namely their desire to gain reelection, so "votes loyal to the judge were easier to cast when one national poll after another found far more Americans, men and women, believed Judge Thomas and not Professor Hill."[9] The lingering question "Who was telling the truth?" was important, but not as a motivation for the voting decisions of most senators. Assessments of this question apparently influenced only a few undecided senators or those whose original support for Thomas was weak. The question of which person to believe was more important to the general public. Assessments of this question clearly divided the American electorate and thereby indirectly influenced the confirmation vote as senators watched the public opinion polls in their home states.

Thomas was ultimately confirmed because a sufficient number of Southern Democrats broke ranks with their party and voted in favor of confirmation. Their decision to vote for Thomas was heavily influenced by the fact that their political survival depends upon the support of African-American voters and African-Americans' support for Thomas was very strong in the South: "A number of Southern Democrats . . . noted privately that black voters in their states backed Thomas. . . . and [they] felt they could not afford to take [a] major stand that was unpopular."[10] Democratic Party strategists feared that senators' votes against Thomas would not only hurt the individual senators, but would hurt the entire Democratic Party with the African-American voters in the South:

In Georgia, black state Democratic Rep. Calvin Smyre, who has organized the statewide campaigns of successful Senate and gubernatorial candidates, says he was particularly afraid that defeat of the Thomas nomination would have resulted in significant black defections from the Democratic Party. "The black community is a little upset [wondering] why these Democrats are taking a black man through this type of process," he says.[11]

Although the process and outcome of the confirmation hearings were thoroughly infused with politics, perceptions about the plausibility of Hill's and Thomas's respective versions of events influenced some senators' votes and contributed to bitter feelings that lingered in the aftermath of the hearings. Any understanding of the consequences of the controversy surrounding this critical nomination requires analysis of two issues. First, what were the flaws in the Judiciary Committee's hearings—hearings that had the putative purpose of discovering the facts surrounding Hill's sexual harassment claim. Second, what were the purported weaknesses in Anita Hill's testimony that her critics claimed made her allegations implausible and unpersuasive. These two issues triggered the electoral consequences of Thomas's critical nomination because segments of the public were thoroughly dissatisfied with the Senate's treatment of Hill's allegations.

Surprise Allegations and Reactive Processes

Clarence Thomas was nominated by President Bush on July 1, 1991 to replace Thurgood Marshall on the Supreme Court. Thomas and his Republican advisors spent the entire summer preparing for the confirmation process by lobbying potential supporters and by studying videotapes of David Souter's confirmation hearings in order to plan his answers to the questions that would inevitably be asked of him by senators. Then, just five days before Thomas's hearings were scheduled to begin on September 10th and unbeknownst to Thomas and his advisors, an investigator for Democratic Sen. Edward Kennedy's Labor and Human Resources Committee called University of Oklahoma law professor, Anita Hill, to ask whether Hill had knowledge of any sexual harassment during Thomas's tenure as Chairman of the Equal Employment Opportunity Commission. Hill asked for more time to consider whether to provide information, but on September 9th she agreed to talk to a former law school classmate who was an aide to Democratic Sen. Howard Metzenbaum. On September 10th and 12th, Hill spoke with her acquaintance as well as to staff members on the Senate Judiciary Committee, who agreed that her information and name would be kept confidential, but persuaded her that if her information was to be used, the Committee members must know her identity.[12] Hill provided the name of Judge Susan Hoerchner, a friend in whom she confided when the alleged harassment occurred, and Hoerchner, a Yale Law School classmate of Hill's, corroborated at least part of Hill's story for the Committee staffers on September 18th, four days after Thomas finished testifying before the Committee. Hill continued to express uncertainty about whether she wanted her name provided to the Committee so that it could investigate the matter and give Thomas an opportunity to respond to the allegations, but on September 23rd she agreed to have her name used and to cooperate with an investigation by the Federal Bureau of Investigation. Two days before the Committee's September 27th scheduled vote on Thomas's nomination, Committee chairman, Sen. Joseph Biden, began to brief Democratic members about the FBI's report on Hill's claims and Clarence Thomas was informed of the allegations. By the day of the Committee's vote, not all members had read the FBI's report and some of the Republican members had not even been briefed about the charges. The vote went forward, a 7–7 deadlock, without a complete examination of Hill's charges.[13] The fact that the Committee went ahead with the vote despite the awareness of several members about Hill's lingering charges led to accusations that the Committee, comprised entirely of males, was insensitive to women's concerns.[14] The responsibility for going forward was shared by all members of the Committee who were aware of the pending allegations:

In what many senators now describe as the biggest mistake of all, no one tried to delay the Sept[ember] 27th [C]ommittee vote, even though any member of the panel could automatically have demanded a week's delay. Nor did anyone [initially] block unanimous consent for the Senate vote to occur on Oct[ober] 8th.[15]

On September 28th, Thomas filed a sworn statement denying Hill's allegations and that appeared to end the matter until, on October 5th, Hill's name and a portion of the FBI's report were leaked to *Newsday* and National Public Radio. With a rising tide of public controversy, Thomas reluctantly requested a delay in the confirmation vote by the full Senate—although it seems likely that the Senate would have delayed the vote anyway because of fears by Republican senators that Thomas's support might slip away.[16] Three days later, on October 11th, the Committee began hearing testimony from Hill, Thomas, and other witnesses concerning the allegations of sexual harassment.

Although the second round of hearings was scheduled immediately in order to avoid unduly delaying the Senate's consideration of the nomination, the short time frame provided little opportunity for thoughtful consideration of how the Committee would conduct these unprecedented hearings in order to best seek the truth about the allegations. Republican senators, such as Thomas's mentor, Sen. John Danforth, argued that no hearings should be held because "the delay and hearings would accomplish nothing [and] in the end the dispute would come to down to whether the senators believed the word of Judge Thomas or the word of Professor Hill."[17] To begin with Danforth's presumption, however, is merely to indicate the obvious fact that many senators who were politically committed to Thomas, as Danforth was, were not likely to believe Hill no matter what evidence she brought forward.

Republican Strategies for One-Sided Adversarialness

The Republicans' strategy from the outset was to attack Anita Hill, an obscure but respected law professor:

The fierce Republican counterattack on Anita F. Hill's testimony sprang from high-level White House consultations among dispirited officials who concluded as the new hearings unfolded that the way to save Judge Clarence Thomas's nomination was to cast doubt on Professor Hill's character and motivation.[18]

Staff members for Republican senators on the Judiciary Committee "furiously dug for dirt on Hill . . . [and] fed information to Sen. Orrin Hatch who used it to imply that Hill had fabricated her story."[19] At the outset, political motivations not only precluded careful consideration of an effective truth-seeking process, but also led Thomas's supporters to evince little genuine curiosity about whether or not Hill might be telling the truth. The Republicans had invested their image, prestige, and future success in the carefully planned nomination of Thomas to replace Thurgood Marshall, and they were apparently not about to suffer a political defeat if there was any way that they could prevent it.

During the hearings, the Republicans designated Sen. Arlen Specter as their lead questioner. Specter, the former Philadelphia district attorney, approached his task in the lawyer's adversarial mode. In the American legal system, lawyers are taught that adversarial proceedings are the most effective method to seek the truth. However, despite Senator Specter's enthusiasm for an adversarial approach, the processes employed by the Judiciary Committee during the hearings did not fit the model of adversarial process that is regarded as a truth-seeking mechanism:

The adversary process assigns to each participant a single function. The judge is to serve as neutral and passive arbiter. Counsel are to act as zealous advocates. According to adversary theory, when each actor performs only a single function the dispute before the court will be resolved in the fairest and most efficient way.[20]

During the Hill-Thomas hearings, Specter and other Republican senators (especially Senators Alan Simpson and Orrin Hatch) were zealous advocates on behalf of Thomas in their attacks on Hill's credibility, but no one zealously argued on Hill's behalf or attacked Thomas's credibility. The Democrats were more restrained in their questioning, and they did not engage in the Republicans' inflammatory tactics and wild theorizing in an effort to discredit Thomas. While Republican senators theorized about Hill's sexual fantasies and Senator Simpson behaved in McCarthy-esque fashion by claiming to possess yet never producing letters purported to provide damaging information about Hill,[21] the Democrats, by contrast, "seemed clueless about what their role in the messy spectacle should be other than to get Hill's testimony on the record."[22] While the Democrats appeared to be intimidated by accusations that they had bungled the investigation, the Republicans "battered the other side by going ugly early and often with nasty personal attacks, by successfully linking the Democrats with liberal advocacy groups and by using volatile images of race."[23] Thus, instead of a true adversarial proceeding in which zealous advocates advance their causes before a neutral jury or a learned judge, the hearings were a one-sided affair in which "[t]he Democrats made a pass at figuring out what happened in the case [and] [t]he Republicans tried to win."[24]

As a result of the one-way adversarialness in a non-adversarial process, "Professor Hill ended up fighting an octopus of charges: That she was an erotomaniac, that she was a ruthless careerist, that she was a disgruntled, vindictive woman, that she was insane and that she was a zombie-like pawn of liberal interest groups."[25] By contrast, because Democrats lacked the Republicans' unity and desire to treat the hearings purely as an adversarial political contest, Thomas was able to avoid the harsh treatment that Hill received. Thomas was successful in recasting the sexual harassment controversy into an issue of racism directed at him by the Democrats and liberal advocacy groups. As scholars subsequently observed:

Thomas once again diverted attention away from the issue at hand. . . . [He] rudely exclaimed that the proceedings are "a high-tech lynching for uppity blacks who in any way deign to think for themselves. . . . [U]nless you kowtow to the old order, this is what will happen to you. You will be lynched, destroyed, caricatured by a committee of the U.S. Senate rather than hung from a tree." Coupled with talk of black male sexual stereotypes, he managed to shift the tide of public sentiments with his appeal to an argument about race.[26]

The Democratic senators, all white males, apparently felt too uncomfortable with a charge of racism coming from an African-American man to counter that charge and thereby present Thomas with the same public challenges that Hill faced from the Republicans.

The Democrats' Failure to Pursue Truth-Seeking Processes

Although Democrats control the Senate Judiciary Committee and therefore had the opportunity to shape significantly the structure of the hearing process, by seeking to accommodate the Republicans' concerns about the fairness of the process to Thomas, the Democrats failed to enhance the truth-seeking potential (albeit limited) of a controversial political event. For example, the hearing process created significant initial advantages for Thomas's position by "allowing the [Bush] administration to set the standard for judgment (Thomas should have the benefit of the doubt) and [by] the timing of Thomas's appearances during the second round of hearings (during prime-time television hours)."[27] There was no compelling reason for the presumption in favor of Thomas that Senator Biden declared should be granted the nominee. The presumption of innocence formally exists in criminal cases because of Americans' concerns about not depriving people of their liberty without proof beyond a reasonable doubt. However, Thomas was not facing a criminal conviction or incarceration. He was responding to an allegation of sexual harassment, which as a *civil* matter in courts, requires a showing only of "a preponderance of evidence." If the allegations were found to be persuasive by the U.S. Senate, the worst thing that would happen to Thomas would be that he would remain a life-tenured judge on the U.S. Court of Appeals for the District of Columbia Circuit. An unnecessary presumption in Thomas's favor, however, could place on the Supreme Court a man who, in a normal sexual harassment case, might have been proven liable by the preponderance of evidence standard for such civil cases.

By permitting Thomas to determine when he would make his presentation to the Committee, Thomas was able to present his case first to a large national television audience and thereby make a favorable impression on public opinion before the details of allegations against him had even been revealed. This was an opportunity to make a significant impact upon the public's and senators' first impressions without having to rebut any specific allegations. Indeed, Thomas used this opportunity to his advantage to place his critics on the defensive by claiming that the allegations of a single African-American woman somehow constituted an issue of racism instead of an issue of sexual harassment.

Because there were apparently few (if any) formal rules about what matters would constitute evidence for the proceedings, the information presented to the Committee (and to the public) was a mishmash of testimony regarding facts and wild speculation about motives that contributed to confusion rather than to elucidation: "Potentially relevant evidence on both sides—Thomas's supposed interest in pornography, Hill's employment records—was ruled off limits. Testimony that never would have made it into court came pouring in. . . . "[28] For example, a central point in Hill's allegations was that Thomas "had given her vivid and unwanted descriptions of pornographic movies that he had seen."[29] Support for the plausibility of this assertion was available because Thomas's friends admitted that he had watched pornographic films:

The supporter and friend [of Judge Thomas's], Lovida H. Coleman, Jr., issued a statement in response to questions about stories circulating in the capital that Judge Thomas had often been a patron of X-rated movie houses while a student at Yale Law School in the early 1970's. Ms. Coleman, also a student at Yale at the time, said that Judge Thomas "at least once humorously described an X-rated film to me and other colleagues." Elaborating beyond the statement, she acknowledged that this had occurred more than once.[30]

Unfortunately for Anita Hill and the public, however, "the Democrats had become so cowed that they failed to question Judge Thomas at all about accounts from his friends about his interest in pornographic films."[31] Instead of admitting probative information, such as Thomas's friends' verification of his involvement with pornography and testimony from sexual harassment experts who might have been able to explain to skeptical senators why victims of sexual harassment might behave as Professor Hill did,[32] the Committee listened to such things as senators asking Thomas's supporters, "who had no reason to know[,] whether it was 'a possibility that Professor Hill imagined or fantasized Judge Thomas saying the things she has charged him with.' "[33] Expert testimony would have given the senators greater perspective concerning whether Hill's delayed charges were plausible:

As it happens, this fit the classic pattern of sexual harassment cases: put the alleged victim on trial. But because the Senate and the White House agreed there would be no expert witnesses, Elizabeth Schneider, a visiting professor at Harvard Law School, said, "The Senators will be evaluating that credibility issue in a total vacuum. We're dealing with people who do not understand the legal requirements for sexual harassment, who do not understand the wealth of study that has been done on this issue."[34]

One senator, who was undecided about how to vote on the Thomas nomination, criticized the Committee for not ordering live testimony from the second woman who alleged, with the support of a corroborating witness, improper sexual conduct by Thomas.[35]

Professor Hill's account was also supported in part by a telephoned statement from another former employee of Judge Thomas, Angela Wright, who said that he had made "inappropriate" remarks about her body when she headed the public affairs office at the Equal Employment Opportunity Commission in 1984 and 1985. "Actually, what he said was, 'What size are your breasts?' " she said in the statement of a conversation that reportedly occurred at a banquet the two attended in 1984.
    Ms. Wright also stated, as has Professor Hill, that Judge Thomas asked her for dates and once showed up unannounced at her apartment. A former co-worker with Ms. Wright, Rose Jourdain, also stated to the committee that Ms. Wright had admitted to her at the time that Judge Thomas's remarks about "her figure, her body, her breasts" had bothered her.[36]

In sum, information was excluded that would have been useful in a truth-seeking process and information was presented that served only to advance groundless, politically motivated speculation intended to raise questions about the plausibility of Hill's allegations.
    The foregoing observations do not imply that the hearings could have been structured differently or would have led to different

results. The political purposes and pressures that motivated the actions of the senators insured that the Senate Judiciary Committee could not even attempt to replicate a structured, truth-seeking judicial proceeding. The purpose of analyzing the hearings is merely to demonstrate that the proceedings were not a truth-seeking process. The partisan maneuvering and efforts to obscure rather than elucidate the truth were obvious to many members of the public. This generated anger among many women, particularly because of the widely held belief that if women had been represented on the Committee, someone would have had the interest and motivation to fight for more emphasis on truth-seeking in the hearing process. The overtly partisan posturing that appeared intended to get the hearings over with quickly, rather than seriously explore the important allegations raised by Hill, struck many women as evidence that the senators, even those Democrats ostensibly in favor of equality for women, were too insensitive and self-interested to genuinely work to protect the interests of women.

THE PLAUSIBILITY OF ANITA HILL'S CLAIMS

A major point that angered many women was the senators' insensitivity to the plausibility of Hill's claims. A recurring theme throughout the sexual harassment hearings was the Republican senators' assertions that Hill's behavior at the time of the alleged harassment and thereafter was inconsistent with the male senators' perceptions about how a harassment victim would act. In order to illuminate this insensitivity perceived by many women and to assess the plausibility of Hill's sexual harassment claim, it is useful to examine the arguments and tactics that were used by Thomas's supporters to cast doubt on Hill's testimony.

A crucial question that apparently puzzled many senators was why Anita Hill did not report the harassment at the time the offensive incidents allegedly occurred. When, according to Hill's testimony, Clarence Thomas spoke to her in graphic and unwanted sexual terms on occasions during her employment as his assistant

from 1981 to 1983, he was engaging in a form of sexual harassment. The traditional view is that sexual harassment constitutes
offensive conduct that is clearly sexual in nature by a person in a
position of authority over the victim.[37] The fact that Hill did not
report the harassment at the time it occurred was cited by several
senators as a key factor that made her story unbelievable. Sen.
Dennis DeConcini, the lone Democrat on the Committee who
supported Thomas, said: "If you're sexually harassed, you ought
to complain, instead of hanging around a long time."[38] Thomas's
strong defender, Sen. Alan K. Simpson, Republican of Wyoming,
said he did not believe Professor Hill could not have found "fertile
ground for her complaint" if she had made it openly in Washington
during the early 1980s.[39] In fact, however, Hill's reluctance to raise
a claim of sexual harassment at the time that the events occurred
is typical of many women's reactions to victimization by forms of
discrimination.

Sexual harassment is very common. Ninety percent of Fortune
500 companies, for example, have dealt with such complaints.[40]
However, many women do not bring forward allegations because
of concerns that nothing will be done about their claims and fears
that they will suffer reprisals for raising the issue. This is true even
of women who work for the federal government:

Yet despite how disturbing and destructive sexual harassment is,
women have had difficulty making complaints, formal or informal,
about the problem. The House Subcommittee that investigated sexual
harassment in the federal government found few women reported sexual
harassment; indeed, of the hundreds of women who called or wrote
directly to the subcommittee, most of them had not filed complaints. A
survey by Federally Employed Women reached the same conclusion
that few women report sexual harassment. Instead women keep quiet
because they fear reprisals, because they believe complaining is useless,
and because they suspect supervisors will treat this deeply troubling
problem as a frivolous complaint. The experiences of those who do
report these problems confirm these suspicions. In the Working
Women's Institute survey, complaining backfired and resulted in retaliation as often as it helped reduce the harassment.[41]

In order for perceived grievances to be addressed through administrative processes or the legal system, they must be transformed by the victim into a complaint that can be processed through available dispute-processing procedures.[42] Discrimination complaints, however, of which sexual harassment constitutes one specific variety, are generally reported at much lower rates than other kinds of grievances. A study of the development of litigation in American society found that relative to other kinds of claims, few discrimination grievances are transformed by victims into actual cases:

The pattern for discrimination grievances is quite different [from other types of claims]. Seven of ten grievants make no claims for redress [to the offending party]. Those who do are likely to have their claim resisted, and most claimants receive nothing. Only a little more than one in ten disputants is aided by a lawyer, and only four in a hundred disputes [that have been voiced to and rejected by the offending party] lead to litigation. [And only eight out of one thousand perceived grievances lead to litigation.] The impression is one of perceived rights which are rarely fully asserted. When they are, they are strongly resisted and pursued without much assistance from lawyers or courts.[43]

The reluctance of discrimination victims to voice their grievances is most clearly revealed by comparing discrimination grievances with other kinds of grievances that provide a basis for civil litigation. In the terminology of civil litigation research, perceived injuries are called grievances. When grievances are voiced to offending parties, they become claims and when the offending party declines to remedy the situation voluntarily, a dispute exists. In order to receive judicial attention, disputes must be brought to lawyers, the actors who transform disputes into legal actions. Lawyers, however, may also discourage the pursuit of grievances and thereby limit the entry of claims into the legal system.[44] As indicated by Table 4–1, according to the findings of litigation research, when discrimination grievances are compared to other kinds of grievances, it is quite clear that there is something different about the nature of discrimination claims that discourages victims

Table 4-1

Patterns of Grievances, Disputes, and Claims Per One Thousand Grievances for Discrimination Cases and for Other Kinds of Civil Cases

	Discrimination	Typical Civil Claim	Tort	Post-Divorce
Grievances	1,000	1,000	1,000	1,000
Claims	294	718	857	879
Disputes	216	449	201	765
Consult Lawyer	29	103	116	588
Court Filings	8	50	38	451

Source: Richard E. Miller and Austin Sarat, "Grievances, Claims, and Disputes: Assessing the Adversary Culture," Law and Society Review 15 (1980-81): 544. Data used by permission of the Law and Society Association.

from coming forward.[45] Obviously, in postdivorce disputes, in which the disputants do not care about any future relationship with each other, grievances are vigorously pursued. Tort grievances are distinguished by the number of claims that are resolved voluntarily or through negotiations when voiced to the offending party. Discrimination grievances, by contrast, are typically held back by the victims, just as Anita Hill failed to immediately pursue any harassment allegations against Thomas at the time the alleged events occurred.

In some discrimination grievances, the victims may lack the necessary information, skills, and resources to pursue a claim. This clearly was not the case for attorney Anita Hill. She knew it was possible to pursue such claims and she had the knowledge and resources to learn how to pursue such a claim within the federal government if she had chosen to do so. Yet, other factors about discrimination cases apply to attorneys, such as Hill, as well as to other victims who feel deterred from raising claims. There is a risk of retaliation if a claim is voiced against a boss. Consistent with these sentiments, Hill claimed that she feared the harassment would lead to retaliation against her. She spoke of her fear of being pushed out of good assignments, losing her job, maybe even not being able to find any job at all within the Reagan administration if she continued to resist Thomas's alleged advances.[46] Moreover, as Richard Miller and Austin Sarat have observed: "There may be some stigma attached to the grievance itself or to the act of assertion. . . . In discrimination grievances, especially, victory may turn to defeat. Those who are assertive, even if vindicated, are branded as troublemakers."[47]

The inefficiency of administrative proceedings may present an additional deterrent to federal employees, such as Anita Hill: "[A]lthough the guidelines of the Equal Employment Opportunity Commission give Government agencies 180 days to resolve a [sexual harassment] case the average claim took 418 days, while the average for complaints from the Departments of Justice and State was more than 1,000 days."[48] In Hill's case, in particular, there was little to be gained by initiating a complaint. As Catherine MacKinnon observed, "It wasn't a good legal bet [for Hill to file a complaint or suit at the time of the harassment]. The main thing you want to do is to stop him from doing it, and apparently he did stop."[49] According to MacKinnon, in the early 1980s courts had not yet recognized that a hostile work environment was enough to constitute sexual harassment. Even if Hill had been able to prove harassment, there was no money to be won. She had not lost her job and so she could not collect compensatory damages, and punitive damages were not available at all under the law at that time.[50] Moreover, studies of discrimination cases indicate that there are significant psychological barriers that hinder victimized people from publicly labeling themselves as victims and thereby risking hostility and retaliation that serve only to reinforce a sense of powerlessness.[51] Such experiences by discrimination victims provide a plausible explanation for why Hill, when first contacted by staffers, wished to avoid controversy by keeping her identity secret. The legitimacy of her fears was ultimately confirmed and even reinforced by the Hill-Thomas hearings when Hill was attacked from every angle by Thomas's supporters. Hill's treatment by the Judiciary Committee subsequently led other women to decline to testify before Congress in separate proceedings concerning gender discrimination.[52]

A further deterrent to inhibit Hill from raising a claim is the fact that "[i]n the American setting, litigation tends to be between parties who are strangers. Either they never had a mutually beneficial continuing relationship . . . or their relationship . . . is ruptured. In either case, there is no anticipated future relationship."[53] Because Hill saw Thomas as someone who could be influential, positively or negatively, on her career prospects, she was reluctant to challenge him with a formal claim. This anticipation of future contacts—which led to occasional telephone and other contacts after she left government service—bewildered Thomas's supporters (or so they said) but was consistent with other women's experiences in seeking advancement (and survival) in male-dominated professional networks.[54]

Senator Specter's Adversarialness in Questioning Hill

Although Republican Sen. Arlen Specter of Pennsylvania claimed that he attempted "to be scrupulously polite and professional and non-argumentative" in questioning Hill,[55] a close examination of his questions indicates that his manner was that of a professional prosecutor seeking to attack Hill's credibility through adversarial, goal-oriented cross-examination. Specter's aggressive approach in attacking Hill's credibility outraged many women and ultimately helped an underdog female candidate win the Democratic primary in the Pennsylvania Senate race to oppose Specter's reelection. Through his questioning, he attempted to show that Hill's story was not plausible because an experienced attorney, Specter's consistent characterization of Hill at the time of the harassment, would have kept notes about the incidents for evidentiary purposes.

By repeatedly characterizing Hill as an experienced attorney at the time of the incidents, Specter appeared to be attempting to achieve his goal of persuading the audience that she must not have been harassed because her behavior was inconsistent with what Specter asserted would be the behavior (i.e., making notes for evidentiary purposes) of an experienced attorney. However, was Hill really an experienced attorney at that time? Hill graduated from law school in 1980 and she worked for Thomas at the Department of Education and the EEOC from 1981 through 1983. She was never an experienced litigator who would have been knowledgeable and concerned about preserving evidence. She was an inexperienced attorney who spent one year as an associate with a large Washington law firm before becoming the assistant to an administrator within federal government agencies. Given the nature of Specter's attempt to enhance if not distort her experience and presumptive knowledge, it is interesting to ponder whether Specter, if he needed legal representation for litigation and sought the services of an experienced attorney, would hire someone only one or two years out of law school?

Specter claimed to be very concerned about the absence of contemporaneous evidence to corroborate the incidents that Hill claimed had occurred. He attempted to create the inference that her failure to make notes for evidentiary purposes indicated that her claim was not plausible. In fact, however, there was contemporaneous evidence of the events: Hill's four corroborating witnesses. Their testimony served precisely the same purpose as any notes that Specter claimed he had expected to see. In fact, their testimony was superior to any notes in that they could place precise dates (years) on the recorded evidence (i.e., the description of Thomas's harassing activities that they heard from Hill) while any notes made by Hill would have been subject to challenge concerning whether they had been manufactured recently in an effort to impress the Senate Committee.

The four corroborating witnesses who testified before the Senate Committee had all been told separately by Hill about the sexual harassment incidents years before Thomas's nomination to the

Supreme Court. Three of the witnesses, a California workers' compensation judge, a project manager for the American Public Welfare Association, and a corporate lawyer for a prominent New York law firm, testified that Hill told them about the sexual harassment at the time that the incidents occurred.[56] The fourth witness, a law professor at American University, heard about the harassment in 1987 when he asked Hill why she left government service. Hill did not volunteer information about the incidents to the two male witnesses (the corporate lawyer and the professor) who were not long-standing friends of hers. They elicited the uncomfortable information by asking her questions when they detected her distress about certain subjects, thus lending credence to the idea that traumatic events had happened to her which she was reluctant to discuss. For example, the corporate lawyer testified that he detected that something was troubling Hill during a telephone conversation when he was dating her in 1983. According to the attorney, who was then a graduate student at Harvard University, "Anita Hill revealed to me that her supervisor was sexually harassing her. . . . I recall that she did not initially volunteer this information; rather, during the telephone conversation, it quickly became clear to me that she was troubled and upset. . . . [She] told me her boss was making sexual advances toward her."[57] The witnesses were apparently credible, since no one effectively attacked the plausibility and veracity of what they said either before or after they testified.

In his prosecutorial style, "Senator Specter pressed hard with the witnesses who told of Professor Hill's accounts of harassment, demanding to know why they had not advised her to leave or protest."[58] Perhaps Specter was attempting to create an inference that they would have taken action if she had really told them these things, but "[e]ach of them said they had not thought it appropriate to offer advice and had not pursued an obviously distraught Professor Hill for details of the harassment she complained of."[59] If Specter had genuinely been interested in the existence of contemporaneous recordings of Hill's allegations, he should have been very impressed by the corroborating witnesses. However, because his efforts were obviously part of a strategy to discredit Hill without regard to the plausibility of her story, he appeared to ignore the corroborating testimony when he reached his ultimate conclusions about Hill's veracity, or rather, the lack thereof.

Specter asserted that contemporaneous notes prepared by Hill would have been "very influential, if not determinative" if Thomas had retaliated against her for initiating a claim against him or for spurning his alleged advances.[60] Despite Hill's concurrence that notes "would be very influential,"[61] was Specter's assertion really accurate? Probably not. If Hill had initiated a claim against Thomas, with or without notes, it would still be her word against his. The incidents of harassment described by Hill always took place with no one else present. If Thomas denied her allegations, as he certainly would have done to avoid fatal damage to his career prospects, who would have been believed? Thomas was the protegé of an influential United States senator, John Danforth, someone for whom Thomas had worked in the Missouri Attorney General's Office and in Congress and someone who had strong protective feelings for Thomas. Thomas had captured the attention of powerful conservative Republicans and, at the EEOC, he was one of the highest ranking African-American officials in the Reagan Administration. By contrast, Hill's only apparent mentor, apart from Thomas, was the lawyer from her old law firm who recommended her to Thomas. It appears, however, that he would have been of little use to Hill in a conflict with this rising political figure (i.e., Thomas) because he was a friend and law school classmate of Thomas's. Indeed, according to Thomas, Hill's sponsor from the law firm was Thomas's dearest friend,[62] hardly the kind of professional connection to protect her in a conflict with Thomas. In the conflicting versions of events, she was not likely to be believed over Thomas. Any notes she kept to record what Thomas said to her would have been attacked as uncorroborated, self-interested fiction created precisely for the purpose of giving the appearance of recorded evidence. If she produced notes after Thomas retaliated against her, it would have looked like an easily manufactured, self-protective measure. At best, she would have been shuffled into a new position elsewhere in government with few prospects for advancement after earning a troublemaker label by making unsubstantiated accusations against a rising star within the Reagan administration. At worst, she would have been frozen out of meaningful assignments or dismissed for poor work performance, just as she feared. Because she gained her law school teaching position at Oral Roberts University, which led to her subsequent position at the University of Oklahoma, through Clarence Thomas's connections and recommendations, she certainly would have had a different career path if she had raised a claim against Thomas.

Specter's putative concern about the production of contemporaneous recordings for evidentiary purposes actually demonstrated his desire to discredit her testimony. Unless Specter was being naive by not recognizing the obvious his-word-against-hers situation that Hill would have faced, the Senator's interest could not have reflected genuine concern about how she might have realistically protected herself from adverse consequences by bringing charges against Thomas when the harassment occurred.

In the final analysis, despite Specter's efforts, Hill's testimony is plausible precisely because she did not raise a claim against Thomas at the time that the harassment occurred. By waiting until she was approached by Senate staffers many years later, the plausibility of Hill's testimony was more powerful because of the existence of credible corroborating witnesses who could serve the contemporaneous recording function that Specter inquired about. She obviously did not manufacture the allegations about Thomas simply to derail his nomination to the Supreme Court because she had told other credible people about the harassment many years before. If she had raised a claim against Thomas when the incidents occurred, the corroborating witnesses' statements could have been dismissed as hearsay manufactured in Hill's self-interest. Because the corroborating witnesses testified years after the events occurred, they confirmed that Hill did not create and had no motive to create claims against Thomas in order to undercut his Supreme Court nomination.

The corroborating witnesses' testimony does not necessarily guarantee that Hill was telling the truth. The possibility still exists that she told these witnesses untrue descriptions of events in the early 1980s, although they obviously found her words and demeanor to be credible for someone enduring harassment. However, the corroborating witnesses, especially when considered in light of the research documenting discrimination victims' reluctance to come forward, effectively make Hill's story very plausible, contrary to the assertions of Specter and Thomas's other politically motivated supporters.

Hill's Motive in Coming Forward When She Did

Thomas's supporters claimed that Hill's charges stemmed from a conspiracy against Thomas's nomination by liberal political interest groups. According to Senator Hatch, "It's what's ruining our country, in large measure. Because some of these groups . . . are vicious."[63] In questioning Thomas during the hearings, Hatch declared, "[A]ll these interest groups have scratched through everything on earth to try and [*sic*] get something on you all over the country. . . . And there's a lot of slick lawyers in those groups— slick lawyers—the worst kind."[64] Hatch went on to quote a *Washington Post* article as his basis for implying that interest groups motivated Hill's accusations against Thomas: "Here is indiscriminate, mean-spirited, mud slinging, supported by the so-called champions of fairness: liberal politicians, unions, civil rights groups, and women's organizations."[65] Thomas himself asserted that Hill was the pawn of "someone, some interest group [that] came up with this story"[66] and Thomas's wife, although explicitly conceding that "I don't have any evidence" to support the conclusion, reiterated this theme of political motivation in her *People* magazine article.[67]

It is undisputed that interest groups mobilized against Thomas's nomination, that they called around the country trying to discover information useful for blocking his nomination, and that they initiated the contact with Anita Hill to inquire about her knowledge of sexual harassment by Thomas at the EEOC. They were undoubtedly quite pleased by the prospect of her testimony about sexual harassment by Thomas. The fact that Thomas's opponents located Hill does not, however, indicate that they controlled her or suggested to Hill what her testimony should be. Hill's initial reluctance to provide information that Thomas's opponents were so eager to have brought forward to the Committee seems to indicate that she was not working for any interest group. In addition, the advisors who assisted Hill during the hearings were not representatives of any organized interest groups opposed to Thomas's nomination, but "were assembled largely from the efforts of a group of women law professors who rushed, on their own, they say, to organize legal talent for [Hill]."[68]

Is there any evidence that Hill had any political motivation to manufacture false allegations against Thomas either for her own political agenda or at the behest of an interest group? No. Just as Thomas's lawyer-wife publicly admitted after his confirmation, there is no evidence to substantiate this claim. Hill's corroborating witnesses, unconnected individuals who are not political activists, provided the most compelling rebuttal to any speculative theorizing about political motivations. As recognized by any knowledgeable trial lawyer, the existence of credible contemporaneous recording concerning an incident precludes the possibility that an allegation about the occurrence of the incident was manufactured at a later date. Because Hill told these other people about the harassment years earlier, she was obviously not making it up in 1991 at the behest of an interest group or for any other political motivation. Thus it is not plausible for Thomas and his supporters to assert that he was victimized by a conspiracy because that conspiracy would have had to have been plotted a decade earlier, before anyone could possibly have predicted that Thomas would later be nominated for the Supreme Court.

Political motivations also seem unlikely because of the apparent congruence of Hill's and Thomas's political beliefs. Hill, like Thomas, was an African-American lawyer working for the Reagan administration at the time when the executive branch of government was accused of dismantling or reducing protections for civil rights. Thus she was aligned with and worked to advance the very same Reagan administration policies that caused many liberals to criticize Thomas. Uncontradicted testimony by one of her corroborating witnesses indicated that she generally supported the conservative policies of the Reagan administration, and that she supported the nomination of conservative Judge Robert Bork to the Supreme Court.[69] Hill's apparent conservatism placed her closer politically to Thomas than to the liberal interest groups that Thomas's supporters claim persuaded her to create false allegations.

Thomas's supporters attempted to provide other purported motivations for Hill's allegations against Thomas:

Judge Thomas's supporters sought last week to raise several possible motives for Professor Hill's decision to bring her explosive testimony to the Judiciary Committee. Through the testimony of Judge Thomas's friends, they cast her as a scorned suitor who had sought revenge; as a bitter opponent of Judge Thomas's views against racial quotas as a remedy for discrimination; as a tool of "slick lawyers" running the liberal opposition to the Thomas nomination; as a gold digger who planned to parlay her celebrity into a book contract, and finally, as emotionally unstable.[70]

None of these theories were supported by any evidence other than speculative statements by Thomas's supporters whose own motivations were clear in their attempts to discredit Hill in order to advance Thomas's nomination. However, because of an absence of substantiating evidence to support these theories (which were apparently components of the Republican senators' strategy of discrediting Hill at all costs) and because Hill's corroborating witnesses cast doubt on other possible motivations for creating a false story, Hill's stated motivations, namely bringing relevant evidence to the Committee in response to queries from staffers, remain quite plausible.

With regard to her motives, Hill's story appears plausible not only because she had no discernible political motives, but also because raising the allegations subjected her to unwanted public attention and hostility. Bringing her allegations to light made Hill subject to myriad personal attacks, but, from the outset, did not provide any prospects of personal gain for Hill. Perhaps this is why she appeared to be so reluctant to discuss the incidents until her name had already been revealed in the press. In any case, the personal cost of her experience seems to diminish the likelihood that she had any ulterior motive.

Hill's Continuing Association with Thomas

Thomas's supporters on the Committee strongly implied that if Hill had truly suffered from harassment by Thomas, she never would have continued to work for him. Thus her move with him from the Department of Education to the EEOC was characterized as incomprehensible by the male senators who attacked her credibility. Senators who were not on the Committee cited this issue as a key element in their decision to vote in favor of Thomas's confirmation.[71]

Is it plausible that someone would continue to work for and stay in touch with a person who was abusive? Yes. Like the failure of discrimination victims to report grievances, the continuation of contacts with victimizers can be affected by the victim's sense of powerlessness. According to Kristin Bumiller's study, discrimination victims "are guided by an ethic of survival that encourages self-sacrifice rather than action."[72] Although senators may claim to find the concept implausible, there are frequent reports about the analogous and more extreme situation of women who continue to stay with abusive husbands and boyfriends. Moreover, in the context of Hill's situation, women may also stay in contact with powerful harassers in order to avoid derailing professional careers. According to Hill's corroborating witness, Judge Susan Hoerchner, "[T]he realities of business and professional life are such that she could not afford to burn that particular bridge behind her, particularly to extend the metaphor, when that bridge is the highest person in her field, and her claim to fame."[73] The senators heard further testimony to that effect, but those who supported Thomas claimed not to understand it. To the working women who observed the hearings, the male senators' detachment from everyday issues faced by female workers was a source of frustration and a catalyst for the political mobilization that followed the hearings.

Senator Specter questioned Hill very closely about the reasons that she gave for moving from the Department of Education to the EEOC. In response, Hill claimed that she stayed in Thomas's employ because the harassment had ceased at the time that he offered her the job at EEOC, so she believed at the time that the episodes were over although they later resumed at the new office. Hill also said that she believed that she would lose her position at the Department of Education when Thomas departed because the new Assistant Secretary would presumably want to hire his own personal assistant. Specter attempted to discredit Hill by showing that she could have kept her job at the Department of Education if she had desired to. Specter had an affidavit from Thomas's successor, Harry Singleton, in which Singleton asserted that he would have retained Hill as his aide. There was no indication, however, that Singleton ever informed Hill of this job offer. Specter's apparent purpose was to assert implicitly that the harassment must not have occurred because she moved to EEOC voluntarily although she did not have to stay in Thomas's employ. Hill maintained all along that Thomas had told her that he could not assure that her employment would continue at the Department of Education:

Sen. Specter: Professor Hill, did you know that as a Class A attorney you could have stayed on at the Department of Education?

Prof. Hill: No I did not. Not at that time.

Sen. Specter: Did you make any effort to find out that as a Class A attorney you could have stayed on at the Department of Education?

Prof. Hill: No, I relied on what I was told.

Sen. Specter: Sorry, I didn't hear you.

Prof. Hill: I relied on what I was told by Clarence Thomas. I relied on what I was told by Clarence Thomas. I did not make further inquiry.

Sen. Specter: And what are you saying that Judge Thomas told you?

Prof. Hill: [The] indication from him was that he could not assure me of a position at Education.[74]

Specter's adversarial style obscured the key issues concerning Hill's veracity and the plausibility of her story. Specter emphasized a retrospective, objective assessment of whether Hill could have kept her position in the Department of Education (i.e., that as a Class A attorney she was entitled to a position). In doing so, he missed the relevant issue, namely a subjective assessment of Hill's knowledge and beliefs at the time that she decided to go to the EEOC with Thomas. Her motives and actions were based upon what she knew at the time she made her decision, not what she might or should have known. Specter paid scant attention to her testimony that the offensive behavior had ceased at that time and, moreover, he mischaracterized the content of Hill's testimony: "And according to [Hill's] statements, . . . she went with him to EEOC in significant part, if not in major part, . . . because she *would have lost her job*" (emphasis supplied).[75] In fact, Hill never stated that she would lose her job, but that *she believed* that she would lose her job. Thus, Specter gave the appearance of discrediting her version of events, but a close examination of his mischaracterization of her statements reveals that his implicit assertions did not detract from the consistency and plausibility of her testimony. Such dogged attacks on her testimony later helped to mobilize women voters against Specter during the 1992 elections.

Senator Specter's Allegation of Perjury

Professor Hill's veracity became a point of contention when Specter "accused [her] of perjuring herself in testimony Friday by giving the committee contradictory statements about whether she had been told by a Senate staff member last month that her account of sexual harassment would force Judge Thomas to withdraw his nomination."[76] Specter continued to repeat and defend his charge of perjury against Hill after the confirmation process ended.[77] In analyzing the following detailed excerpt of Hill's testimony to assess her veracity, one underlying factor must be kept in mind. Specter was the key inquisitor for a Republican strategy developed for attacking Hill's credibility before she had even presented her testimony. As described by the *New York Times*:

The Republicans had gone to work last week, before Hill even testified, trying to rip at her character with a thousand cuts. The Justice Department, the Equal Employment Opportunity Commission, White House lawyers and lobbyists, and some of the smartest, most acid-tongued Senators did not try so much to rebut her specific charges as to offer elaborate theories of how and why she might be lying or delusional. They tried to sew doubt about her character and shift the contest from her versus him to him versus the process.[78]

In advancing the preplanned strategy, Specter's questioning of Hill adopted the adversarial techniques of cross-examination. Not only did Specter, at times, mischaracterize Hill's statements, but as commentators have observed about the goals of cross-examination, Specter sought to find or manufacture some statement that he could seize upon to claim that she lacked credibility. As Judge Marvin Frankel has written in his critique of the legal system, "[T]he skillful cross-examiner, whose assignment is to win, not merely or necessarily to arrive at truth[,] ... employ[s] ancient and modern tricks to make a truthful witness look like a liar."[79] Throughout Hill's morning testimony, Specter focused repeatedly and exclusively on the question whether Hill had been told that Thomas *would* (i.e, definitely) withdraw *upon her mere allegations* (i.e., just by publicly stating her charges). Hill consistently answered no to these questions. Specter was obviously trying to get Hill to make an admission that he could use to declare that her allegations were motivated by an expectation that public accusations of sexual harassment would force Thomas to withdraw his nomination. In the afternoon, Hill stated that she was told that Thomas *might* (i.e., possibly) withdraw as one of many possible outcomes *after the Senate undertook proceedings to investigate her charges* (i.e., based upon the Senate's actions, not Hill's alone). Although Hill was addressing two different questions in these statements regarding both the probability (i.e., definitely versus possibly) and timing (i.e., upon mere allegations versus after Senate action) of a possible withdrawal by Thomas from the nomination process, Specter labeled these statements as inconsistent and used them to trumpet a charge of perjury in an attempt to attack Hill's credibility. The words with emphasis supplied in the testimony highlight the fact that Hill and Specter were talking about different probability and timing regarding what Hill was told by Senate staffers with respect to the possibility of Thomas withdrawing:

Round I: Morning Testimony

Sen. Specter: Professor Hill, the *USA Today* reported on October 9th "Anita Hill was told by Senate staffers if she signed an affidavit alleging sexual harassment by Clarence Thomas. Anita Hill was told by Senate staffers her signed affidavit alleging sexual harassment by Clarence Thomas would be the instrument that 'quietly and behind the scenes' *would force him to* withdraw his name." Was *USA Today* correct on that, attributing it to a man named Mr. Keith Henderson, a ten-year friend of Hill and former Senate Judiciary Committee staffer?

Prof. Hill: I do not recall. I guess, did I say this? I don't understand who said what.

Sen. Specter: Let me go on. He said, Keith Hill, Keith Henderson, a ten-year friend of Hill and former Senate Judiciary Committee staffer, says Hill was advised by senators' staffers that the charge would be kept secret and her name kept public, kept from public scrutiny "they would["]—apparently referring again to Mr. Henderson's statement —"approach Judge Thomas with the information and he *would withdraw* and not turn this into a big story."

Henderson says. Did anybody ever tell you that by providing the statement that there would be a move to press Judge Thomas to withdraw his nomination?

Prof. Hill: I don't recall any story about pressing, using this to press anyone.

Sen. Specter: Do you recall anything at all about anything related to that?

Prof. Hill: I think that, I was told that my statement would be *shown* to Judge Thomas. And I agreed to that.

Sen. Specter: But was there any suggestion, however slight, that the statement with these serious charges *would result in withdrawal* so that it wouldn't have to be necessary for your identity to be known or for you to come forward under circumstances like these?

Prof. Hill: There was no, not that I recall. I don't recall anything being said about him being pressed to resign.

Sen. Specter: Well, this would only have happened within the course of the past month or so. Because all this started just in early September.

Prof. Hill: Sure. I understand.

Sen. Specter: So that when you say that you don't recall, I would ask you to search your memory along this point. Perhaps we might begin—and this is an important subject—about the initiation of this entire matter in respect to the senate staffers who talked to you. But that's going to be too long for the few minutes that I have left, so I would just ask you once again, you say you don't recollect, whether there was anything at all said to you by anyone, that, as *USA Today* reports, that just by having the allegations of sexual harassment by Clarence Thomas that it would be the instrument that "quietly and behind the scenes" *would force him to withdraw* his name. Anything related to that in any way whatsoever?

Prof. Hill: The only thing that I can think of, if you check, there were a lot of phone conversations, we were discussing this matter very carefully. And at some point there might have been a conversation about *what might happen*. There might have been, but, I don't remember the specific kind of comments about quietly and behind the scenes pressing him to withdraw.

Sen. Specter: Well, aside from quietly and behind the scenes pressing him to withdraw, any suggestion that just the charges themselves in writing *would result* in Judge Thomas withdrawing, going away?

Prof. Hill: No. No. I don't recall that at all. No.

Sen. Specter: Well, you started to say that there might have been some conversation. . . .

Prof. Hill: There might have been some conversation about what *could possibly* occur.

Sen. Specter: Well, tell me about that conversation.

Prof. Hill: Well, I can't really tell you any more than what, I discussed what the alternatives were, what might happen with this affidavit that I submitted. We talked about a possibility of the Senate committee coming back for more information. We talked about the possibility of the FBI asking, going through the FBI and getting more information. Some questions from individual senators. I just, the statement that you're referring to, I really can't verify.

Sen. Specter: Well, when you talk about the Senate coming back for more information, the FBI coming back for more information, senators coming back for more information, that has nothing to do at all with Judge Thomas withdrawing. So that when you testified a few moments ago that there might possibly have been a conversation in response to my question about the possible withdrawal—I would press you on that, Professor Hill, in this context, you testified with some specificity about what happened ten years ago. I would ask you to press your recollections about what happened within the last month.

Prof. Hill: And I have done that, Senator. And I don't recall that comment. I do recall that there *might have been some suggestion* that if the FBI did the investigation, that the Senate might get involved, that there may be, that a number of things *might occur*. But I really, I have to be honest with you. I cannot verify the statement that you are asking me to verify. There's not really more that I can tell you on that.

Sen. Specter: Well, when you say a number of things might occur, what sort of things?

Prof. Hill: May I just add this one thing?

Sen. Specter: Yes.

Prof. Hill: The nature of that kind of conversation that you're talking about is very different than the nature of the conversations that I recall. The conversations that I recall were much more vivid. They were more explicit. The conversations that I have had with the staff over the last few days in particular have become more blurry, much more blurry. But these are vivid events that I recall from even eight years ago, when they happened. And they are going to stand out much more in my mind than a telephone conversation. They were one-on-one personal conversations as a matter of fact, and that adds to why they are much more easily recalled. I am sure that there are some comments that I do not recall the exact nature of from that period as well. But these here are the ones that I do recall.

Sen. Specter: Professor Hill, I can understand why you say that these comments, alleged comments, stand out in your mind. We've gone over those and I don't want to go over them again. But when you talk about the withdrawal of a Supreme Court nominee, you're talking about something that is very, very vivid, stark. And you're talking about something that occurred within the past four or five weeks. And my question goes to a very dramatic and important event if a mere allegation *would pressure a nominee to withdraw* from the Supreme Court, I would suggest to you that that's not something that wouldn't stick in a mind for four or five weeks, if it happened.

Prof. Hill: Well, Senator, I would suggest to you that for me these are more than mere allegations. So that if that comment were made—these are the truth to me, these comments are the truth to me—and if it were made, then I may not, I may not respond to it the same way that you do.

Sen. Specter: Well, I'm not, I'm not questioning your statement when I use the word allegations to refer to ten years ago. I just don't want to talk about it as a fact because so far, that's something we have to decide. So I'm not, not stressing that aspect of the question. I do with respect to the time period. But the point that I would come back to for just one more minute would be, well, let me ask it to you this way. Would you not consider it a matter of real importance if someone said to you, Professor, you won't have to go public, your name won't have to be disclosed, you won't have to do anything, just sign the affidavit and this man, as the *USA Today* report, would be the instrument that "quietly and behind the scenes" *would force him to withdraw* his name. Now, I'm not asking you whether it happened. I'm asking you now only if it did happen, whether that would be the kind of statement to you which would be important and impress upon that you would remember in the course of four or five weeks.

[*PAUSE while Prof. Hill appears perplexed by the question and turns to consult with her advisors*].

Prof. Hill: I don't recall a specific statement. I cannot say whether that comment would have stuck in my mind. I really cannot say that.

Sen. Specter: The sequence with the staffers is very involved, so I'm going to move to another subject now. But I want to come back to this and over the luncheon break I would ask you to think about it further. If there's any way you can shed any further light on this question because I think it is an important one.

Prof. Hill: Thank you.

Round II: Afternoon Testimony

Sen. Specter: I want to finish the chronology if I may, Professor Hill. When my time expired, we were up to the contact you had with Mr. Brudney on September 9. If you could proceed from there to recount who called you and what those conversations consisted of as it led to your coming forward on, coming forward to the Committee.

Prof. Hill: We discussed a number of different issues. We discussed, one, what he knew about the law of sexual harassment. We discussed what he knew about the process for bringing information forward to the Committee. In the course of our conversation, Mr. Brudney asked me what, for specifics about what it was that I, what I had experienced. In addition, we talked about the process for going forward. What *might happen* if I did bring information to the Committee. That included that an investigation might take place. That some, I might be questioned about the Committee in closed session. It even included something to the effect that the information might be presented to the candidate or to the White House. There was some indication that the candidate, excuse me, the nominee *might not* wish to continue the process.

Sen. Specter: Mr. Brudney said to you that the nominee, Judge Thomas, *might not* wish to continue the process if you came forward with a statement on the factors that you testified about.

Prof. Hill: Well, I'm not sure that that's exactly what he said. I think what he said was, depending on an investigation, the Senate, whether the Senate went into closed session and so forth, it *might be* that he would not wish to continue the process.

Sen. Specter: So Mr. Brudney *did* tell you that Judge Thomas *might not* wish to continue to go forward with his nomination if you came forward.

Prof. Hill: Yes.

Sen. Specter: Isn't that somewhat different from your testimony this morning?

Prof. Hill: My testimony this morning was about my response to the *USA* newspaper report. And the newspaper report suggested that by making the allegation that that would be enough. That the candidate *would* quietly, and somehow withdraw from the process. So no, I do not believe that it is at variance. We talked about a number of different options, but there was never suggested that just by alleging incidents that that might, that that *would cause* the candidate or the nominee to withdraw.

Sen. Specter: Well, what more could you do than make allegations as to what you said occurred?

Prof. Hill: I cannot do more, anymore, but this body could.

Sen. Specter: Well, but I'm now looking at your distinguishing what you have just testified to from what you testified to this morning. This morning I had asked you about just one sentence from the *USA Today* news. "Anita Hill was told by Senate staffers that her signed affidavit alleging sexual harassment by Clarence Thomas would be the instrument that quietly and behind the scenes *would force* him to withdraw his name.["] And now you're testifying that Mr. Brudney said that if you came forward and made representations as to what you said happened between you and Judge Thomas that Judge Thomas *might withdraw* his nomination.

Prof. Hill: Well, I guess, Senator, that the difference in what you're saying and what I'm saying is that that quote seems to indicate that there would be no intermediate steps in the process. What we were talking about is process. What *could happen* along the way. What were the possibilities. Would there be a full hearing? Would there be questioning from the FBI? Would there be questioning by some individual members from the Senate? We were not talking about or even speculating that simply alleging this *would cause* someone to withdraw.

Sen. Specter: Well, if your answer now turns on process, all I can say is that it would have been much shorter had you said at the outset that Mr. Brudney told you that if you came forward Judge Thomas *might* withdraw. That is the essence, isn't it, of what occurred.

Prof. Hill: No it is not. I think we differ on our interpretation of what I said.

Sen. Specter: What am I, what am I missing here, Professor Hill?

Sen. Edward Kennedy, Democrat of Massachusetts: Let the witness speak in her own words rather than having words put in her mouth.

Sen. Specter: Mr. Chairman, I object to that. I object to that vociferously. I'm asking questions here. If Senator Kennedy has anything to say, let him participate in this hearing.

Sen. Joseph Biden, Democrat of Delaware and Chairman of the Judiciary Committee: [Rapping the gavel softly] Everybody calm down. Professor Hill, give your interpretation to what was asked by the Senator, if you would and then he can ask you further questions.

Prof. Hill: My interpretation. . . .

Sen. Strom Thurmond, Republican of South Carolina: Speak into your machines so we can all hear you in the back.

Prof. Hill: I understood Mr. Specter's question to be what kind of conversation did I have regarding this information. I was attempting in talking to the staff to understand how the information would be used. What I would have to do. What *might be* the outcome of the investigation. We talked about a number of possibilities. But there was never any indication that by simply making these allegations that the nominee *would withdraw* from the process. No one ever said that. I did not say that anyone ever said that. We talked about making, the form that the statement would come in. We talked about the process that might be undertaken post-statement and we talked the possibilities of outcomes. And included in that possibility of outcomes was that the Committee could decide to review the points and that the nomination, the vote could continue as it did.

Sen. Specter: So that at some point in process Judge Thomas *might withdraw.*

Prof. Hill: Again I would have to respectfully say that is not what I said. That was one of the possibilities. But it would not come from simple, my simply making an allegation.

Sen. Specter: Professor Hill, was that what you meant when you said earlier, as best I could write it down, that you controlled it so it would not get to this point.

Prof. Hill: Pardon me?

Sen. Specter: Is that what you meant when you responded earlier to Senator Biden that the situation would be controlled "so that it would not get to this point["] in the hearings.

Prof. Hill: Of a public hearing? In entering into this conversation with the staff member, what I was trying to do was control this information, yes, so that it would not get to this point.

Sen. Specter: Thank you very much.[80]

Giving Specter the benefit of the doubt, perhaps he believed that his original question effectively asked Hill to describe everything that was said to her related to Thomas's possible actions in response to her allegations. However, the way he phrased the question and his follow up question were justifiably perceived by Hill, given his choice of verbs (i.e., "*would* force him"; "*would* result"), as inquiring whether someone told her that Thomas would definitely withdraw. To that question, her answer was a consistent no.

A national newsmagazine declared that Hill "seemed . . . evasive" during her questioning by Specter.[81] According to the news magazine's description,

Specter pressed her to recall discussing such a scenario [in which her allegations would force Thomas to withdraw] with anyone. First she demurred that she did not recall that specific comment. Pressed again, she allowed, "There might have been some conversation about what could possibly occur." On Saturday Specter quickly attacked Hill's change in testimony as "flat-out perjury."[82]

A careful reading of the testimony reveals, however, that this news account shares Specter's error declaring that Hill changed her testimony. Specter's initial and consistent questioning did not ask her whether anyone talked to her about what *might happen*; he consistently used the verb "*would*" in asking about what was said in conversations. Her responses to his questions were consistent in both the morning and the afternoon (i.e., no one said what would happen; someone speculated about what might happen). In common parlance, the conclusion that her testimony was completely consistent might appear to be a hypertechnical justification based upon semantics (i.e., distinguishing between what she was told about what would happen versus what she was told about what might happen)—and perhaps that is how it appeared to newsmagazines and some segments of the general public. But this was a cross-examination of one lawyer by another in which the participants presumably chose their words carefully. Hill was obviously cautious in resisting Specter's efforts to push her responses in a direction favorable to his preferred outcome and that may be a basis for labeling her as evasive for not telling him everything about all conversations when he embarked upon his questions concerning the *USA Today* article. However, her responses to his specific questions were completely consistent. Although her responses were narrowly tailored to address the questions he asked, the complete consistency of her responses refutes Specter's perjury charge and the implication that this testimony casts doubt upon her veracity.

Specter told Hill that the hearings "would have been shorter had you said at the outset that Mr. Brudney told you that if you came forward Judge Thomas might withdraw." The blame, however, rests with Specter. In his dogged and unsuccessful pursuit of an admission that she expected Thomas to resign when her allegations were revealed, he did not pursue general questioning about what Mr. Brudney said or about what anyone said about what might happen. In the morning session, he always asked what she was told about what would happen and Hill responded to the specific questions that he asked.

With respect to the long-term consequences of Thomas's critical nomination, few people will remember the perjury allegation or its basis. For female voters who were skeptical of Thomas's denials and the Republican senators' adversarial approach, however, Specter's prosecutorial performance and subsequent allegations about Hill's veracity reinforced the anger at the male senators' insensitivity to issues of gender discrimination and sexual harassment.

Other Allegations about Hill's Veracity

Senator Hatch strongly implied that Hill was not truthful because her allegations about specific sexual comments made by Thomas coincided precisely with publicly available sexual material contained in a popular novel, *The Exorcist*. As described in one news report, "Waving a copy of *The Exorcist* before Judge Thomas, Senator Hatch recounted what Professor Hill had testified was the 'oddest episode,' when, she said, the nominee asked her, 'Who has put pubic hair in my Coke?' With a disgusted look, Senator Hatch read from the novel [a passage in which the identical question was posed by a character in the book.]"[83] Hatch also referred to a 1988 legal case to imply that Hill's specific allegations about Thomas were manufactured from other sources.

Today, with his questions, Senator Hatch, suggested that Professor Hill with the possible collusion of interest groups, was manufacturing charges.

In her testimony Friday, Professor Hill said that Judge Thomas made references to her about a movie called "Long Dong Silver. . . . "

Senator Hatch advanced his own theory. Apologizing for the language, he read from a Federal district court case, Carter v. Sedgwick County, Kan., [705 F. Supp. 1474 (D. Kan. 1988)] in which the plaintiff accused the defendant of presenting her with a picture of "Long Dong Silver,"—[a photo of a nude African-American man].

"I'm sure it's available there at the law school in Oklahoma," Senator Hatch said. "And it's a sexual harassment case."[84]

It is possible that Hill created the details of the harassment by copying them from these available sources because her corroborating witnesses could attest only to her general allegation of harassment that was made prior to the cited case. They could not confirm all of the specific statements that Hill attributed to Thomas. Not surprisingly, Hatch did not mention that it is equally plausible that Clarence Thomas drew from these sources in the sexual statements that he made to Hill. *The Exorcist* was published in the early 1970s, well before Thomas met Hill. The 1988 legal case was based on material from a pornographic film and even Thomas's friends admitted that he viewed such films. As the *New York Times* noted, "one need not be familiar with the 1988 case to know about the pornographic character. . . . Long Dong Silver was the stage name of a well-known black actor who made pornographic films as far back as 12 years ago."[85] Moreover, although Hill testified in detail about her harassment and how she came to raise these allegations to the Committee, Thomas was the one who avoided providing complete information. As described in one news report,

Mr. Thomas has angrily stated on several occasions that he will not talk about his private life in the hearing, trying to head off any questions about published reports by his friends and supporters that he was often a patron of X-rated movie houses while a student at Yale Law School in the early 1970's and that he would sometimes humorously describe the pornographic movies to his friends and colleagues.[86]

Because Hatch's theory about borrowing sexual material from other sources could plausibly apply to either Hill or Thomas but lacked substantiation for application to either one, Hatch's theorizing added nothing to the determination of whether Hill or Thomas was telling the truth. Hatch's assertions did not, contrary to his intentions, provide evidence that challenged Hill's veracity. Observant members of the public who were skeptical about the Republicans' motives could, however, become angrier at such tactics based on one-sided, accusatory speculation.

Hill was never permitted to respond to Hatch's charges about the source of the sexually explicit language or his allegations about her collusion with interest groups because he raised these matters *after* she completed her testimony. Despite the fact that these and other attacks (i.e., the perjury claim) were not answered in front of the television klieg lights, her antagonists were unsuccessful in their attempts to substantiate the questions that they raised about her veracity. The Republican senators did, however, reinforce the growing anger of skeptical women voters who believed that the male domination of the Senate led to such apparently unfair, insensitive, and one-sided attacks on a credible, respectable woman.

THE MALE-DOMINATED SENATE AND
WOMEN VOTERS

As detailed in the foregoing sections of this chapter, a close examination of Hill's claims and the purported weaknesses in her testimony demonstrate that her version of events is plausible and that there is no evidence that she lied at any time throughout the entire proceeding. Can the same be said of Clarence Thomas and his supporters? No. The diversionary public show that Senator Specter and his like-minded colleagues performed in purporting to search for inconsistencies and inaccuracies in Anita Hill's statements was noticeably absent when it came to their consideration of Clarence Thomas's testimony and the background of his nomination. As described in Chapter 3, Thomas's evasiveness during his original confirmation hearings reached the point of implausibility when he denied ever discussing the abortion issue with anyone. Yet, because of their partisan loyalties and conservative policy preferences, the same senators who attacked Anita Hill with such vigor failed to give any critical scrutiny to Clarence Thomas. Alone among the Republican senators, Senator Specter questioned Thomas closely on several subjects. It appeared, however, that after voting to recommend Thomas's confirmation, Specter had made such a thorough commitment to the Thomas nomination that he attacked Hill's allegations vigorously instead of reexamining the veracity of Thomas's original testimony.

Thomas's testimony at the hearings concerning Anita Hill's allegation consisted primarily of angry, indignant denials. If he was merely indignant and angry as he categorically denied the charges, little could be concluded about his veracity except that her corroborating witnesses had provided a strong case for the plausibility of her story and made it virtually impossible for him to refute her version of events. Thomas had his own witnesses and despite their attacks on Hill's character, they obviously could not provide probative information concerning Thomas's private conversations with Hill. Thomas's persuasiveness rested on his own testimony and on the assistance he received from his supporters on the Committee who attacked Hill's credibility.

Thomas's own testimony was troubling primarily for its use of hyperbole calculated to change the focus of the hearings. Thomas claimed, for example, that he was being subjected to a high-tech lynching because he was an African-American and a political conservative. He portrayed himself, in the words of one *New York Times* columnist, "with self-pity, as a victim of racial politics"[87] despite the fact, as his wife later admitted, that there was no evidence of a political conspiracy underlying Hill's harassment charge. The use of the term lynching may have "successfully injected the race issue, thereby placing the all-white-male Judiciary Committee and most of the rest of the Senate in a defensive if not retiring posture,"[88] but it effectively trivialized an element of America's violent history of racism. In actual lynchings, people were tortured, mutilated, and killed. In Thomas's case, a vote against him would have left him as a life-tenured judge on the U.S. Court of Appeals—hardly a comparable result. Moreover, Thomas's indignant claim of racism contradicted his previous public statements in which he criticized other African-American leaders for constantly attributing all of their problems to racism. Although the use of hyperbole does not, *ipso facto*, demonstrate a lack of veracity, its use raises questions about what someone is willing to say in order to attain a desired goal. Was Clarence Thomas willing to say almost anything in order to become a Supreme Court justice? A journalist for *Newsday* reported that Thomas admitted as much to a Bush administration official at the time of his hearings.[89]

With respect to longer term political consequences, by playing the race card as a means to deter close examination by the all-white Judiciary Committee, Thomas distracted attention away from the underlying issues of gender discrimination that were really at the heart of Hill's claims. Because Hill was an African-American woman, her allegations were not plausibly based on racism. Yet race is such a potent concept, that by merely raising the issue, Thomas obscured the issue of the treatment of women in the workplace.

This strategy helped to gain confirmation for Thomas but it also incensed many women who felt that the senators had completely neglected the actual issues that should have been the focus of questioning by the Committee. Harriett Woods, the president of the National Women's Political Caucus noted that the clubbiness of the male-dominated Senate served to breed insensitivity to outsiders, especially women. According to Woods, many women were offended that senators were prepared to take Thomas at his word without giving Hill similar consideration: "John Danforth is a Yale man who can stand up and say, according to the rules of this club, 'I've asked the gentleman if he committed the crime and he said no. He's a friend of mine. He's a gentleman. And we should take his word.' That's the way it always was in this club."[90] This dissatisfaction with the Senate's performance in examining Thomas's fitness for judicial office, especially in light of Hill's plausible allegations, motivated women to contribute money to and vote for female candidates as a means to gain greater female representation in the country's highly unrepresentative legislative bodies, most notably the U.S. Senate. The Senate contained only 2 female senators among its 100 members at the time of the confirmation hearing and neither of these women senators were on the Judiciary Committee. As Chapter 5 will discuss, the Thomas nomination constituted a critical judicial nomination because it mobilized a segment of the electorate to seek greater representativeness in government. Many female voters, especially professional and other working women, viewed the Thomas hearings as demonstrating beyond a doubt that the male-dominated Senate was incapable of acting with sensitivity to address issues of concern to women.

NOTES

1. For example, Priscilla Painton, "Woman Power," *Time*, 28 October 1991, 24.

2. David A. Kaplan, "Anatomy of a Debacle," *Newsweek*, 21 October 1991, 26.

3. For example, Jill Smolowe, "He Said, She Said," *Time*, 21 October 1991, 36.

4. Eloise Salholz, "Dividing Lines," *Newsweek*, 28 October 1991, 24.

5. Richard L. Berke, "Support for Thomas Inches Toward Approval in Senate," *N.Y. Times*, 4 October 1991, A16.

6. Richard L. Berke, "Vote on Thomas Is Put Off As Senate Backing Erodes Over Harassment Charge," *N.Y. Times*, 9 October 1991, A1.

7. Richard L. Berke, "3 Senators Who Switched Tell of Political Torment," *N.Y. Times*, 16 October 1991, A13.

8. Adam Clymer, "Senate's Futile Search for Safe Ground," *N.Y. Times*, 16 October 1991, A1.

9. Ibid., A14.

10. R. W. Apple, "Senate Confirms Thomas, 52–48, Ending Week of Bitter Battle; 'Time for Healing,' Judge Says," *N.Y. Times*, 16 October 1991, A13.

11. Thomas B. Edsall and E.J. Dionne, Jr., "The Vote That Split the Liberal Core," *Washington Post National Weekly Edition*, 21–27 October 1991, 12.

12. "How Anita Hill's Allegations Came to Light," *Time*, 21 October 1991, 51.

13. Ibid.

14. Clifford Kraus, "Biden, Champion of Women's Rights, Now Finds His Sensitivity Questioned," *N.Y. Times*, 11 October 1991, A12.

15. Helen Dewar, "The Democrats Went from Bad to Botched," *Washington Post National Weekly Edition*, 28 October–3 November, 1991, 7.

16. For example, Adam Clymer, "After 100 Days, the Hardest Yet for One Senator," *N.Y. Times*, 9 October 1991, A12; Adam Clymer, "Delaying the Vote: How Senators Reached Accord," *N.Y. Times*, 10 October 1991, A11.

17. Clymer, "After 100 Days," A12.

18. Andrew Rosenthal, "White House Role in Thomas Defense," *N.Y. Times*, 14 October 1991, A1.

19. Ann McDaniel, "The Attack of the Bush Men," *Newsweek*, 28 October 1991, 26.

20. Stephan Landsman, *Readings on Adversarial Justice: The American Approach to Adjudication* (St. Paul, Minn.: West Publishing, 1988), 35.

21. For example, Eleanor Clift, "Taking the Low Road," *Newsweek*, 26 October 1991, 30; David E. Rosenbaum, "Simpson Refuses to Make

Public Letters He Says Criticize Hill," *N.Y. Times*, 14 October 1991, A17.

22. Ruth Marcus and Dan Balz, "The Fact-Finding Mission That Became a Slugfest," *Washington Post National Weekly Edition*, 21–27 October 1991, 12.

23. Maureen Dowd, "Getting Nasty Early Helps G.O.P. Gain Edge on Thomas," *N.Y. Times*, 15 October 1991.

24. Ibid.

25. Ibid., A10.

26. Albert P. Melone, Alan R. Morris, and Marc-George Pufong, "Too Little Advice, Senatorial Responsibility, and Confirmation Politics," *Judicature* 75 (1992): 189.

27. Dewar, "The Democrats Went from Bad to Botched," 7.

28. Marcus and Balz, "The Fact-Finding Mission," 13.

29. Michael Wines, "Stark Conflict Marks Account Given by Thomas and Professor," *N.Y. Times*, 10 October 1991, A10.

30. Ibid.

31. Dowd, "Getting Nasty Early," A10.

32. Ibid.

33. Marcus and Balz, "The Fact-Finding Mission," 13.

34. Andrew Rosenthal, "A Terrible Wrong Has Been Done, but to Whom?," *N.Y. Times*, 13 October 1991, E5.

35. Clifford Kraus, "On Eve of Vote on Thomas, a Senator Grapples for Answers," *N.Y. Times*, 15 October 1991, A10.

36. Michael Wines, "Evidence on Who Is Telling the Truth as Senate Takes Up Thomas Debate," *N.Y. Times*, 15 October 1991, A12.

37. Wendy Pollack, "Sexual Harassment: Women's Experience vs. Legal Definitions," *Harvard Women's Law Journal* 13 (1990): 46.

38. Anthony Lewis, "Wages of Cynicism," *N.Y. Times*, 11 October 1991, A15.

39. Adam Clymer, "Parade of Witnesses Support Hill's Story, Thomas's Integrity," *N.Y. Times*, 14 October 1991.

40. Janice Castro, "Sexual Harassment: A Guide," *Time*, 20 January 1992, 37.

41. Jill Laurie Goodman, "Sexual Harassment: Some Observations on the Distance Travelled and the Distance Yet to Go," *Capital University Law Review* 10 (1981): 457. *See also* Karen De Witt, "As Harassment Drama Plays, Many U.S. Employees Live It," *N.Y. Times*, 13 October 1991, 9.

42. William L. F. Felstiner, Richard L. Abel and Austin Sarat, "The Emergence and Transformation of Disputes: Naming, Blaming, Claiming . . . ," *Law and Society Review* 15 (1980–81): 633–37.

43. Richard E. Miller and Austin Sarat, "Grievances, Claims, and Disputes: Assessing the Adversary Culture," *Law and Society Review* 15(1980–81): 545.

44. Marc Galanter, "Reading the Landscape of Disputes: What We Know and Don't Know (and Think We Know) About Our Allegedly Contentious Society," *U.C.L.A. Law Review* 31 (1983): 13.

45. Miller and Sarat, "Grievances, Claims, and Disputes," 544.

46. Smolowe, "He Said," 39.

47. Miller and Sarat, "Grievances, Claims, and Disputes," 541.

48. Martin Tolchin, "Citing Thomas Hearings, Women Refuse to Testify," *N.Y. Times*, 24 October 1991, A10.

49. "Hill's Accusations Ring True to a Legal Trailblazer," *Detroit Free Press*, 13 October 1991.

50. Ibid.

51. Kristin Bumiller, "Victims in the Shadow of the Law: A Critique of the Model of Legal Protection," *Signs: Journal of Women in Culture and Society* 12 (1987): 436–39.

52. "Fear of Frying," *Time*, 4 November 1991, 18; Tolchin, "Citing Thomas Hearings, Women Refuse to Testify," A10.

53. Galanter, "Reading the Landscape of Disputes," 24–25.

54. *See* Marie C. Wilson, "Just a Day at the Office," *N.Y. Times*, 11 October 1991, A15.

55. "Excerpts From Senate's Hearings on the Thomas Nomination," *N.Y. Times*, 13 October 1991, 13.

56. Clymer, "Parade of Witnesses," A10.

57. Ibid.

58. Ibid.

59. Ibid.

60. Testimony of Anita Hill before Senate Judiciary Committee, 11 October 1991 (transcribed by author from audio tape of live broadcast on COURT TV Cable network).

61. Ibid.

62. "Excerpts From the Senate's Hearings on the Thomas Nomination," 10.

63. Ibid., 12.

64. Ibid.

65. Ibid.

66. Maureen Dowd, "Taboo Issues of Sex and Race Explode in Glare of Hearing," *N.Y. Times*, 13 October 1991.

67. Virginia Lamp Thomas, "Breaking Silence," *People*, 11 November 1991.

68. Neil A. Lewis, "Hill Advisers Say They Took the Initiative to Help," *N.Y. Times*, 15 October 1991, A11.

69. "Questions to Those Who Corroborated Hill Account," *N.Y. Times*, 14 October 1991, A13.

70. Wines, "Evidence on Who Is Telling the Truth," A12.

71. For example, Dowd, "Getting Nasty Early Helps," A10.

72. Bumiller, "Victims in the Shadow of the Law," 438.

73. "Questions to Those Who Corroborated Hill Account," A14.

74. Testimony of Anita Hill before Senate Judiciary Committee, 11 October 1991 (transcribed by author from audio tape of live broadcast on COURT TV cable television network).

75. Ibid.

76. Richard L. Berke, "Thomas Backers Attack Hill; Judge, Vowing He Won't Quit, Says He Is Victim of Race Stigma," *N.Y. Times*, 13 October 1991, 1.

77. Gwen Ifill, "A Split Decision on Specter's Role," *N.Y. Times*, 21 October 1991, A14.

78. Dowd, "Getting Nasty Early Helps," A10.

79. Marvin Frankel, *Partisan Justice* (New York: Hill & Wang, 1978), 16.

80. Testimony of Anita Hill before Senate Judiciary Committee, 11 October 1991 (transcribed by author from audio tape of live broadcast on COURT TV cable television network).

81. Smolowe, "He Said," 40.

82. Ibid.

83. Berke, "Thomas Backers Attack Hill," 9.

84. Ibid.

85. Neil A. Lewis, "Judge's Backers Seek to Undercut Hill," *N.Y. Times*, 13 October 1991, 8.

86. Dowd, "Taboo Issues of Sex and Race," 9.

87. James Reston, "More Than Just Up or Down," *N.Y. Times*, 15 October 1991, A15.

88. Melone, Morris and Pufong, "Too Little Advice," 189.

89. Timothy M. Phelps and Helen Winternitz, *Capitol Games* (New York: Hyperion, 1992), 178.

90. Maureen Dowd, "7 House Women March to Senate in Attempt to Delay Thomas Vote," *N.Y. Times*, Oct. 9, 1991, A11.

5

Political Mobilization in the Aftermath of the Thomas Nomination Controversy

Many women felt outraged by the Clarence Thomas confirmation hearings. They were especially appalled by the Republicans' concerted attacks on Anita Hill's credibility as the hapless Democrats sat idly by. Although public opinion polls initially indicated that a majority of Americans, including many women, disbelieved Anita Hill's sexual harassment claims,[1] the hearings touched a special nerve with educated, affluent, and working women, the categories most inclined to become politically active. According to a *Los Angeles Times* survey, individuals with some postgraduate education were more likely than people with lower educational levels to have believed Anita Hill's charges (50 percent vs. 35 percent).[2] As expressed by one former congressional press secretary in the immediate aftermath of the hearings, "[O]ne of the very difficult things for both Democrats and Republicans coming out of this is that activist women—women who support candidates, who donate money, who donate time—they by and large, in overwhelming numbers, supported Anita Hill."[3] Over time, Hill's credibility attracted support from a wider range of the American public. A *Wall Street Journal*/ABC News poll found that although people believed Clarence Thomas over Anita Hill (40 percent to 24 percent) in October 1991 when the hearings ended, by September

1992, public opinion favored Hill over Thomas (44 percent to 34 percent).[4]

Hill raised the issue of sexual harassment in the workplace, a pervasive problem in offices and factories throughout the country that is unrecognized and misunderstood by many men. The problem of sexual harassment is very real, however, for working women. For example, a 1992 survey found that 60 percent of female lawyers had experienced sexual discrimination or harassment at the hands of male judges and male lawyers,[5] legal professionals who are supposedly trained to understand such concepts as discrimination and equal protection under the law. In the year following Hill's televised testimony, a record number of sexual harassment claims (7,407), representing a 50 percent increase over the previous year, were filed with the federal Equal Employment Opportunity Commission.[6] When Anita Hill raised claims that many women could understand, senators on the Judiciary Committee not only failed to listen to her story, they attacked and fabricated wild theories about her presumed sexual fantasies. The Republican senators who attacked Professor Hill presumably believed that they were fulfilling their responsibilities as partisan politicians in fending off her allegations that threatened to derail their President's controversial nominee for the Supreme Court. In the eyes of many women, however, the televised hearings projected the stark image of a lone woman facing interrogation by hostile, all-male committee members who appeared incapable of understanding the pervasive elements of gender bias that confront American women on a daily basis. Although women constitute a majority of the country's population, there were only two women among the one hundred members of the U.S. Senate (Barbara Mikulski, D-Maryland; Nancy Kassebaum, R-Kansas—a third, the widow of North Dakota Senator Quentin Burdick was appointed to serve out her late husband's term in 1992) and these women were not members of the Judiciary Committee. Thus the political mobilization and change generated by Thomas's critical nomination was not caused by the appointment of Clarence Thomas *per se*; women reacted to the insensitivity and unrepresentativeness of the U.S. Senate as demonstrated by the all-male Judiciary Committee's treatment of Anita Hill's allegations. Moreover, although women constituted the core of the campaign contributors and voters mobilized by the Senate's actions in the Thomas hearings, by September 1992 a national survey revealed that 47 percent of Americans believed that the Senate did not treat Professor Hill fairly and respectfully.[7]

WOMEN IN AMERICAN ELECTORAL POLITICS

For most of American history, formal legal barriers precluded active participation by women in electoral politics.[8] Most importantly, women were denied the right to vote in most states until the third decade of the twentieth century. Women's political organizations formed after the Civil War to attempt to secure the right to vote for women. The most important organization, the National American Women's Suffrage Association (NAWSA), was formed in 1890 when other groups merged in order to create a single organization.[9] In the 1890s, Wyoming, Colorado, Utah, and Idaho granted women the right to vote, but little progress was made on the issue in other states until 1910. The NAWSA grew from a membership of 13,000 members in 1893 to a membership of two million in 1917 and its substantial growth in support coincided with successful efforts to enfranchise women in a dozen additional states before 1920.[10] By the time the Nineteenth Amendment was added to the Constitution on August 26, 1920, the constitutional amendment which finally granted to women the right to vote nationally, advocates of women's suffrage had battled through "56 referendum campaigns, 480 efforts to get state legislatures to allow suffrage referenda, 47 campaigns at state constitutional conventions for suffrage, 277 attempts to include woman suffrage in state party programs, and 19 campaigns to get the Nineteenth Amendment through Congress."[11] Obviously, the struggle to gain electoral participation was long and difficult.

Access to participation in elections did not, however, translate into discernible political power for women. Many women did not exercise their right to vote. Many others, having been socialized into a role as subordinate to their husbands and other men, did not seek to develop and exercise independent viewpoints. In addition, women voters did not cast their ballots as a bloc. They were as divided as men when assessing election issues and choosing candidates. Moreover, because of the generally accepted view that women were supposed to remain at home as wives and mothers, there were few opportunities for women to seek real political power as successful candidates for important public offices.[12] Although women gradually became more involved in politics, some women successfully gained influential political offices, and women's organizations lobbied effectively on a variety of issues, it was not until the 1970s that women began to assert themselves as an identifiable voting bloc with identifiable interests. According to Ethel Klein, it was "[t]he efforts of feminist activists to sensitize the public on women's issues [that] led to the emergence of a feminist vote in 1972."[13]

Many changes had occurred in American society to facilitate the development of women voters as a force, albeit sometimes a modest one, in political campaigns and elections. Changes in technology and the availability of products, such as the development of electric appliances, convenient foods, and supermarkets, freed women from many of the daily chores that consumed their mothers' and grandmothers' lives in caring for children and families. Instead of spending all of their time cooking, cleaning, and sewing, many women had reason to enter higher education to pursue careers. Advancements in birth control technology, especially the Pill, diminished married women's prospects for the previously inevitable series of pregnancies that kept women in earlier eras from leaving their roles as full-time mothers and homemakers. During the 1960s, as the nation witnessed African-Americans' struggle for equality, many women and men increasingly recognized the lack of equality enjoyed by women. As Congress finally produced legislation to combat racial discrimination, it also wrote laws to secure equal pay for women and provide protections against gender discrimination in employment. The Women's Movement raised issues concerning equality and thereby helped to diminish legal and attitudinal barriers to women's integration into higher education, professions, and the workforce generally. In the 1970s, gender discrimination remained pervasive in virtually every aspect of American life, but as women made inroads into a variety of institutional settings, formal recognition of the problems of gender bias and inequality began to grow.

The 1970s witnessed an expansion of women's involvement in the major American political parties. This expanded participation was partly the result of reform efforts, such as the Democrats' new rules to diversify demographic representation at party conventions, but, according to M. Kent Jennings, it was also "fed by structural changes such as delayed age of marriage, lower birth rates, and much greater female participation in the work force."[14] Societal changes facilitated new opportunities for women to participate in political organizations. As women became increasingly integrated as participants in electoral politics, they had the potential to influence electoral outcomes. In the 1976 presidential election, for example, "[w]omen played a critical role in Carter's victory over Ford, because Carter received 49.7 percent of men's votes and 51.3 percent of women's votes" within an electorate containing a female majority among registered voters.[15]

Political Consciousness and Voting Behavior

Despite the fact that party identification rather than gender is usually the strongest determinant of a voter's choice in casting a ballot, a greater consciousness of women's issues during the 1970s increased the salience of those issues for many individual citizens making decisions in voting booths. In 1976, "[a]lthough most people did not see feminism as an issue in [the presidential campaign], some men (30 percent) and some women (32 percent) preferred one candidate over the other on the basis of . . . the candidates' positions on [gender] role equality and the likelihood that [the candidates] would promote policies of benefit to women as a group."[16] In the 1980 presidential election, the voting decisions of some women were influenced by consideration of a major issue of interest: ratification of the Equal Rights Amendment (ERA). The Democratic Party endorsed the Amendment, although President Jimmy Carter was criticized for putting forth inadequate efforts to secure enactment. By contrast, the Republican Party and its candidate, Ronald Reagan, opposed the ERA. According to Klein, "women who favored the ERA and saw Carter as a supporter of sex equality solidly cast their votes for him."[17]

Although many male voters supported the ERA and were sympathetic to issues of special concern to women, women voters were much more likely to make such concerns determinative of their voting decisions:

Men's support for the ERA and preference for Carter's position on sex equality did not have a significant influence on their vote. . . . They, unlike women, did not punish Reagan for opposing ERA. This difference in the importance of women's rights issues on men's and women's votes, particularly during an election in which sex equality was a central campaign issue, illustrated that once women's consciousness was raised, women's political evaluations were filtered through feminist concerns. In contrast, men's sympathy for women's rights did not impinge on their political decisions because men, who do not confront sexism in their daily lives, felt that other issues were more important.[18]

Just as Klein's research concerning presidential elections from 1972 through 1980 identified the importance of women's "consciousness [about gender inequality] in the political mobilization and maintenance of underrepresented groups,"[19] the political mobilization of female candidates and voters in reaction to the 1991 Thomas nomination hearings confirmed the same phenomenon. Many women were angered by the disturbing and disappointing actions of the all-male Judiciary Committee members who mishandled Anita Hill's allegations. Because of their consciousness about gender bias and the salience of that consciousness to their political behavior, these women actively supported female candidates for the U.S. Senate and other offices, even, in some cases, if it meant deviating from their traditional political party loyalties.

Some political scientists have argued that "women have had a relatively low sense of self-worth and tend to undervalue their own [political] competence, they have been far too dependent upon and trustful of other authorities, especially their husbands."[20] Thus, according to Virginia Sapiro, a "feminist consciousness" involves shedding an unduly trusting outlook by gaining an awareness of barriers facing women. This awareness can provide motivation for political action seeking change.[21] The Thomas nomination controversy provided an important catalytic moment for many women to solidify, in Sapiro's phrase, their "feminist consciousness" in order to seek an end to the male-monopoly over decision making in the Senate and other governmental institutions. For example, Rep. Patricia Schroeder (D-Colorado) confirmed this source of women's political mobilization in commenting on the success of female candidates during the 1992 election campaigns in the aftermath of the Thomas nomination. According to Schroeder,

For a long time I think women trusted politicians they thought were listening to their issues and understood. . . . That's what the Anita Hill hearing was all about. It was, "Oh, my God, we trusted these guys and they're clueless." I think women have thrown up their hands and said, "Enough." There is real distrust.[22]

In many elections, although women may be more inclined than men to support Democratic candidates, the basis for women's voting decisions is not unlike that of men in that voters' choices are determined by such factors as political party affiliation and concerns about the economy.[23] However, like the ERA issue in 1980, which Klein found as an important motivation for some women's voting choices,[24] the Thomas nomination provided a specific focus for women's political consciousness and mobilization during the 1992 elections. In fact, Thomas's critical judicial nomination comes much closer to fulfilling what Carol Mueller characterized as "[t]he dream of the suffragists and the nightmare of the political bosses[:] . . . a women's voting bloc that would introduce new issues, new candidates, new directions into the familiar political calculations."[25] The ERA issue motivated voters' choices between candidates, especially the male presidential candidates, who would support (or oppose—depending on one's view of the ERA) equal legal rights for women. By contrast, the catalytic Thomas hearings mobilized women voters to support female candidates for a variety of political offices on the premise that women officeholders would make new kinds of decisions in shaping the entire range of policies and programs that are subject to governmental influence and control. Thus the election of new kinds of candidates as a result of the critical Thomas nomination has much broader implications for changes in politics and policy than did earlier political mobilizations addressing specific issues, such as the ERA.

POLITICAL MOBILIZATION IN U.S. SENATE RACES

Although many women disagreed with President Bush's nomination of Clarence Thomas and feared the threat that Thomas's nomination posed to abortion rights and other legal issues, the focus of political mobilization generated by the Thomas hearings was the male-dominated Senate's unrepresentativeness and insensitivity to women's issues. In the immediate aftermath of Thomas's confirmation, major contributors to the Democratic party announced that they would not assist any of the eleven Democratic senators who voted to confirm Thomas and the Democratic Senatorial Campaign Committee was abandoned by its liberal direct-mail consultants.[26] Despite the strong immediate reactions against the Democratic senators who voted for Thomas and thereby, in effect, expressed disbelief about Hill's testimony, there were questions about whether the Thomas nomination controversy would significantly impact the 1992 elections. As expressed by one national newsmagazine, "political episodes, however searing at the time, have a remarkably short shelf life . . . [so] it is not clear who will actually remember or what lessons they will take away from the Hill-Thomas hearings."[27] One year later, however, it was clear that the Thomas nomination controversy remained on the minds of candidates and voters as an unprecedented number of women—eleven—were major party candidates for U.S. Senate seats in the general election: Barbara Boxer (D-California); Carol Moseley Braun (D-Illinois); Dianne Feinstein (D-California); Charlene Haar (R-South Dakota); Jean Lloyd-Jones (D-Iowa); Sen. Barbara Mikulski (D-Maryland); Patty Murray (D-Washington); Gloria O'Dell (D-Kansas); Geri Rothman-Serot (D-Missouri); Claire Sargent (D-Arizona); and Lynn Yeakel (D-Pennsylvania).[28] There would likely have been a twelfth candidate, former Democratic vice-presidential candidate Geraldine Ferraro in New York's Senate race, if a second female candidate, former U.S. Rep. Elizabeth Holtzman, had not won 13 percent of the vote and thereby contributed to Ferraro's one percentage point primary election loss to State Attorney General Robert Abrams.[29] Not only did the news media label the Thomas-Hill hearings as the biggest reason for the successful emergence of women candidates,[30] the candidates also pointed to the Thomas nomination controversy as a catalytic event for themselves and their supporters. The momentum of female candidates was maintained in the general election when Mikulski gained reelection and four other women won Senate seats.

Carol Moseley Braun and the Illinois Senate Race

Carol Moseley Braun, an African-American attorney serving in the relatively obscure office of Cook County Register of Deeds, shocked the political establishment when she defeated incumbent Sen. Alan Dixon in the Illinois senatorial primary.[31] Braun was recruited to run in the aftermath of the Thomas nomination hearings because Dixon alienated many liberals within his party by being one of the few northern Democrats to vote in favor of Thomas's confirmation.[32] Braun declared her candidacy a few days after the confirmation vote on Thomas. According to Braun, the hearings motivated her to run. As she weighed the possibility of entering the race, people began calling to encourage her to throw her hat in the ring: "As it got worse and worse, as the Senate hearings became more of an embarrass-ment, more calls and letters were coming. . . . By the time I got requests from white males in Republican counties in downstate Illinois, I knew something was up."[33] Moreover, the Thomas-Hill hearings demonstrated to Braun, as they did to many other women, that the Senate's unrepresentative composition had to be changed: "We all thought of the Senate as this lofty place, a Valhalla even, where weighty decisions were made by these serious men. . . . Instead, we saw that they were just garden-va-riety politicians making bad speeches. We need to open up the Senate to the voices that have been excluded."[34]

Although Braun had few campaign funds or organizational resources, she benefitted from a three-way battle that primarily pitted Senator Dixon against a millionaire male challenger, neither of whom apparently regarded Braun as a serious threat until it was too late. Braun captured 38 percent of the vote while Dixon gained 35 percent and the third candidate won only 27 percent.[35] The impact of the Thomas nomination in mobilizing women was apparent because Braun "even carried conservative suburban areas around Chicago, apparently gaining crossover votes from Repub-lican women."[36] According to exit polls, Braun won 62 percent of the votes of white suburban women who said Thomas should not have been confirmed, while Dixon gained support from only 10 percent of such voters.[37] Thus affluent female suburbanites, the kinds of voters who often favor Republican candidates, provided strong support for Braun.

Braun continued to emphasize women voters' disgust with the Thomas-Hill hearings as she campaigned during the general elec-tion. For example, in her solicitation letter to potential contributors throughout the United States, Braun presented her message in large letters *on the outside of the envelope*, presumably so that her motivations would be clear even to those who normally discard the multitude of election-year solicitation letters without opening them. Although the solicitation letter inside the envelope discussed a range of issues from the defense budget to pollution control to health care, the excerpt on the envelope focused solely on the Thomas nomination:

LAST FALL, THE BEST KEPT SECRET IN WASHINGTON WAS EX-POSED. . . . The hearings on the Clarence Thomas nomination gave us all a rude awakening. Of the 100 members of the United States Senate, the most important legislative body in the country, 98 are men. Women constitute only 2% of these decision-makers. . . . The outcome of the Thomas hearings would have been different had there been women—or even *one* woman—on the Judiciary Committee. But, as we watched the hearings day in and day out, the questions we wanted to ask . . . the issues we thought should be addressed never surfaced. *WE DIDN'T HAVE A VOICE.* (emphasis in original)

Braun's appeals apparently reached a broad, interested audience because during the second quarter of 1992 she raised more money than any other Senate candidate.[38]

Braun ultimately became the first female African-American in the U.S. Senate when she won the November general election by garnering 53 percent of the vote. Women voters, 58 percent of whom voted for Braun, were especially important in her historic victory.[39] She also won 43 percent of the vote in suburban districts that were usually Republican strongholds.[40]

Lynn Yeakel and the Pennsylvania Senate Race

Lynn Yeakel, the affluent, fifty-year-old daughter of a former congressman, was the little-known president of a charity organization for women and children when the Thomas-Hill hearings motivated her to enter the senatorial primary. Although she began her campaign only a little more than two months before the primary, this political novice scored a stunning upset over the state's lieutenant governor who was the Democratic establishment's endorsed candidate in the primary.[41] Yeakel pointed to the Thomas nomination hearings as the primary motivation for her effort to unseat incumbent Sen. Arlen Specter, the Republicans' chief inquisitor of Anita Hill. According to Yeakel, "I looked at those 14 men [on the Judiciary Committee], and particularly at my senator, Arlen Specter, and I thought: These are not the people I want running my life and my children's and grandchildren's lives."[42] Yeakel, who personally experienced sex discrimination when denied a job with an advertising firm in 1965 because of her gender, said that the Thomas "hearings brought home to me that the U.S. Senate is not representative of the U.S. population."[43]

According to news reports, Yeakel "electrified Pennsylvania's otherwise turned-off electorate" with a television advertisement "that opened with Specter grilling Hill and then switched to Yeakel, who asked, 'Did this make you as mad as it made me? I'm Lynn Yeakel and it's time we did something about the mess in Washington.' "[44] Her television advertising campaign, financed by $200,000 of her own money and even more money from a successful fundraising campaign, captured the attention of both Republicans and Democrats. Yeakel received overwhelming support from women and from educated voters, both male and female.[45] Exit polling on primary election day indicated that many Republicans intended to desert their party's candidate, Senator Specter, in the general election: only 60 percent of Republican voters said that they would support Specter in a race against Yeakel.[46]

During the general election campaign, the front of the envelope containing Yeakel's national fundraising solicitation letter had a picture of Senator Specter speaking during the Thomas-Hill hearings. Inscribed in large red letters below Specter's picture were the words, "A cold slap in the face. . . . " Not surprisingly, the solicitation letter itself began by condemning Specter's behavior during the Thomas-Hill hearings:

It was a low point for the United States Senate and a cold slap in the face to women in Pennsylvania and across America.

I've never been more shocked, outraged, and embarrassed than when I watched *Pennsylvania's senior senator browbeat Professor Anita Hill on national television.*

Arlen Specter completely ignored the courage and integrity this woman showed in coming forward with revelations of sexual harassment.

He reverted to his old prosecutor's role to "put her away" in a zealous attempt to save the troubled nomination of Clarence Thomas. . . .

Arlen Specter knew exactly what he was doing and why. (emphasis in original)

The remainder of the letter discussed health care, abortion, the defense budget, and other issues with a continual emphasis on Specter's insensitivity to problems affecting women as evidenced by his support for Thomas's nomination.

According to the *Wall Street Journal*, "Sen. Specter . . . found it necessary to all but grovel in apology for his performance at the hearings."[47] One of his television ads featured the widow of Pennsylvania's late Sen. John Heinz saying, "I certainly didn't agree with Arlen Specter during the Clarence Thomas hearings. . . . Nevertheless, I'm supporting him."[48]

Ultimately, Yeakel gained 49 percent of the vote in the general election and barely lost to the incumbent senator.[49] After the election, political analysts credited Specter with running a textbook campaign that outspent Yeakel by $4 million to overcome his initial deficit and retain his seat.[50] By contrast, Yeakel's inexperienced campaign staff was criticized for blowing the election through strategic errors, such as delaying broadcast of effective television commercials during the general election.[51] Although he won, Senator Specter acknowledged that he had been affected by the Thomas nomination hearings. Specter called the Thomas hearings a "historic event in American history and American culture . . . [which] were a learning experience for me, and perhaps for the country."[52]

Other Senate Races

In California, both Senate seats were open due to the retirement of Sen. Alan Cranston and Sen. Pete Wilson's mid-term election as Governor of California. Former San Francisco Mayor Dianne Feinstein was favored to win one primary and, in fact, won. According to the *New York Times*, Feinstein was "[n]ever considered a special friend to women and now [is] campaigning as a feminist."[53] News accounts implicitly attributed Feinstein's change in emphasis to the tremendous increase in gender consciousness among women voters in the aftermath of the Thomas confirmation hearings.[54] Feinstein used the Thomas hearings in her fund-raising letter as a means to attract support from outraged women and liberal voters:

Dear Friend, I will never forget the weekend of October 11. It was sad and painful to all of us who care about the role of women in our society. The sense of rage I felt as I watched what they did to Anita Hill has not subsided with the passage of time. I am sure you feel the same.[55]

Feinstein won the general election with a commanding 17–point victory over her opponent. Although she easily won the Senate seat with a majority of men's votes, her large margin of victory was attributable to the whopping 26–point advantage that she enjoyed over her opponent among women voters.[56]

In the second primary, Rep. Barbara Boxer, a liberal member of Congress, won an upset victory over the heavily favored male lieutenant governor and a male member of Congress who heavily outspent her on television advertising.[57] Boxer's successful primary campaign was dependent on the support of women. Among women voters, she had a twenty-eight-point edge over the lieutenant governor and, while her opponents attracted individual contributions at the maximum allowable $1,000 level, "[t]wo-thirds of Boxer's contributions came from women, and more than 60 percent were raised in small contributions that averaged $28."[58] Boxer's victory was especially surprising because newspapers reported that "[m]any analysts sa[id] her Senate bid [was] doomed" after revelations that she was among the dozens of members of Congress who bounced checks at the House of Representatives' private bank.[59]

From the outset of the Thomas-Hill controversy, Boxer had been an outspoken critic of the Senate Judiciary Committee's handling of the sexual harassment allegations. Boxer was among seven female members of the House of Representatives who made a highly-publicized march on the Senate when Hill's allegations first emerged in order to demand that the senators stop the confirmation proceedings until the issue was examined.[60] The seven protestors were featured in a front-page photograph in the *New York Times*[61] and Boxer was quoted in national news accounts about how senators refused to discuss the issue with their female colleagues from the House:

> When a contingent of seven House members marched down the marble halls of the Senate to the Democratic caucus room to ask for a meeting about sexual harassment, they were told they couldn't come in. Said California Congresswoman Barbara Boxer: "What could be more symbolic than a closed door?"[62]

The assertiveness of Boxer and her colleagues touched an immediate nerve with women on Capitol Hill who were concerned about the Senate's insensitivity to issues affecting women: "Female staff members in [congressional] offices came out to call 'Right on!' as Representative [Louise] Slaughter and Patricia Schroeder and their female colleagues went on their lobbying rounds [at the Senate]."[63] Apparently such consciousness among female voters in California helped Boxer because the *New York Times* reported that her "[c]ampaign [was] helped by [the] Clarence Thomas hearings and [the] famous photo of Boxer leading [the] charge of women [from the House of Representatives] up [the] steps of [the] Capitol."[64] Boxer reported that she received a tremendous outpouring of financial support within days after the Thomas hearings.[65] Interestingly, Boxer did not emphasize the Thomas-Hill hearings in her national solicitation letter that outlined her many differences with her opponent over public policy issues. However, her letter did criticize her Republican opponent for being anti-women's rights. According to Boxer's fund raising letter, her opponent was quoted in the *Sacramento Bee* as saying, "I would vote for Clarence Thomas just like that! He would make a superb associate justice of the Supreme Court."

In the general election, Boxer completed the women's sweep of California's Senate seats with a 48–42 percent victory that rested on the majority support she received from female voters.[66]

In Washington State's Senate primary, Patty Murray, an obscure state legislator who described herself as "just a mom in tennis shoes," outpolled all other candidates, both Democrats and Republicans, to win the Democratic nomination.[67] While she campaigned as an outsider concerned about a variety of liberal issues of interest to women, Murray made use of references to the Thomas nomination hearings to encourage voters to support her bid to add greater diversity to the U.S. Senate. "I've watched women come into politics thinking they had to become a man to succeed. . . . What I am is a different role model. This mom in tennis shoes is what I really am. I didn't see anything like me during the Clarence Thomas hearings."[68] Murray added that "Anita Hill has changed the face of American politics this year. . . . Millions of women have been motivated by that vision on our TV set."[69] In the general election, Murray won a decisive 10–point victory over her opponent by gaining the support of two-thirds of Washington's women voters.[70]

The national mailing by the Women's Council of the Democratic Senatorial Campaign Committee, issued under the name of Sen. Barbara Mikulski of Maryland, an incumbent seeking reelection, used the Thomas hearings as an example of the insensitivity and the unrepresentativeness of the male-dominated Senate: "That [lack of representation for women] was evident to American women when they saw Anita Hill being interrogated by the all-male Senate Judiciary Committee." The letter cited the need for financial support for Braun, Yeakel, Feinstein, and Boxer, as well as for the Democratic candidate in Iowa who was challenging a

Republican member of the Judiciary Committee: "*And in Iowa, we must stand behind State Senator Jean Lloyd-Jones, who is waging a serious challenge against Republican Senator Charles Grassley—another Anita Hill interrogator*" (emphasis in original). The Democratic National Committee's newsletter similarly emphasized the Thomas nomination hearings in describing the success of female candidates in the primaries: "Galvanized by the courage of Anita Hill, Democratic women have emerged as leaders during the primaries. As a record number of women run for elected office, they have developed the essential grassroots and fundraising support typically enjoyed in years past by only the politically established men."[71] Thus the Thomas nomination hearings were exploited by women candidates and their supporters who clearly viewed the controversy as a useful catalyst for political mobilization against male Republican Senate candidates.

This strategy of using the Thomas-Hill hearings to mobilize support was fed not only by the success of female candidates in senatorial primary elections, but also by the surge in campaign donations triggered by the hearings. Within days after Thomas's confirmation, for example, "Ellen Malcolm, head of EMILY's List, which raises funds for Democratic women candidates, said, 'My phones are ringing off the hook from women and men who are determined to elect more women in 1992.' "[72] EMILY's List (which stands for Early Money Is Like Yeast) received a 50 percent increase in donations in the two months following the hearings. It raised $1.5 million in 1990 and had only 3,500 members at the time of the Thomas hearings in 1991. One year later, it had 22,000 members and had raised $4.5 million for distribution to women candidates in the 1992 election.[73] Most importantly, much of the new money coming in to EMILY's List was donated by women who were not previously known as political activists.[74] During the summer of 1992, the Democratic Party set new monthly fundraising records in July and August,[75] but there is no way to know how much was attributable to the momentum of women's political mobilization and how much was due to optimism about Bill Clinton's prospects for winning the presidential election.

THE CONSEQUENCES OF POLITICAL MOBILIZATION

The catalytic effect of Clarence Thomas's critical judicial nomination extended beyond the success of female candidates for the
U.S. Senate. Women candidates for other offices also benefitted
from the momentum of women's political mobilization and the
media attention directed at the surprising success of women candidates. For example, as of March 1992, before many states had
held their primary elections, there were 109 women running for
seats in the House of Representatives and the number of women
seeking city and state legislative offices in California had at least
doubled since the 1990 election.[76] A woman, Deborah Arneson,
shocked the New Hampshire political establishment by winning
the Democratic gubernatorial primary. Even more shocking to
New Hampshire's political traditions, she advocated a state income
tax, a policy position previously considered fatal to the prospects
of candidates for statewide office there. Apparently, Arneson's
campaign benefitted from the visibility of women candidates that
was generated, at least in part, by the Thomas hearings:

Ms. Arneson acknowledged that in the past few months the growing
interest nationwide in female candidates has probably helped her. . . .
But when she began running more than a year ago, she said, "being a
woman was a liability. . . . Now it's helping us."[77]

By contributing to women's political mobilization, to the success of new candidates, and to governmental attention to policy
issues of special interest to women, Thomas's critical judicial
nomination advanced, in Mueller's words, "[t]he dream of the
suffragists and the nightmare of the political bosses."[78] Those
political leaders and candidates who felt threatened by the emergence of women as competitors for political power found themselves scrambling for ways to react to these new developments. In
one of the more dim-witted reactions to the success of female
candidates in 1992, the former chairman of the Pennsylvania
Democratic Party remarked that the women candidates "seemed

to be saying, 'Here, I've got breasts. Vote for me.' "[79] Claire Sargent, the female candidate for U.S. Senate in Arizona who was running against incumbent Republican John McCain, fired back by saying, "Some of our opponents say we're running on a slogan of 'I've got breasts. Vote for me.' Well, I think it's about time we voted for senators with breasts. . . . After all, we've been voting for boobs long enough."[80] Other women candidates, however, were not able to respond effectively to the rumors and mudslinging that they faced as part of a backlash against women candidates. Gloria O'Dell, the Democratic opponent of incumbent Senator Robert Dole of Kansas, had to fend off fictitious charges that she was a homosexual.[81] Sue Myrick, a loser in the Republican senatorial primary in North Carolina,

maintains that she was defeated by a phone and mail campaign by her opponent's supporters, who charged her with everything from practicing Satanism to having an abortion, an illegitimate child and a homosexual son. [According to Myrick,] "Everything was a lie. If I had been a male, they couldn't have gotten away with any of this. People would have dismissed it." [82]

Other women candidates faced such things as rumors about affairs with political associates and hecklers calling them femi-Nazis and lesbians.[83]

Political success has its costs when established interests are threatened. Do these actions in the 1992 election indicate that women are becoming fully integrated into electoral politics? Alternatively, are female candidates more susceptible to certain kinds of political attacks? The unanswered question after Thomas's critical judicial nomination will be whether female candidates simply face the same mudslinging as male candidates or whether they are subject to especially detrimental smears because their opponents attack them with zeal and the public is more inclined to believe slanderous rumors about women.

The political mobilization of women also began to affect the statements and decisions by elected officials. For example, in the

Senate's pre-election vote to confirm a Bush-appointee to the
federal appellate bench despite the nominee's reputation for insensitivity to the problems of racial discrimination in death penalty
sentencing, Sen. Arlen Specter switched his vote. Specter favored
the nominee in the Judiciary Committee in May, but he became the
only Republican to vote against the nominee when the full Senate
voted in September. According to the *New York Times*:

> The only Republican to oppose Mr. Carnes was Senator Arlen Specter,
> a Pennsylvania Republican who is facing a tough re-election challenge
> from Lynn Yeakel. Mr. Specter is considered vulnerable because many
> of his supporters, particularly women, were angered by his harsh ques-
> tioning last fall of Prof. Anita Hill. . . .
>   . . . In his statement today, Mr. Specter said he had changed his mind
> after a review of the record of Mr. Carnes in several death penalty cases.
> He did not mention that Ms. Yeakel, his Democratic opponent, had
> forcefully raised the issue of the Carnes nomination. . . . [84]

Similar strategic vote switching to avoid the wrath of mobilized
women voters was apparent when the Senate violated its own
informal agreement to protect defense spending by voting 89 to 4
to cut $200 million from military projects and use $185 million of
it for breast cancer research.[85] Medical research funding for
women's illnesses became a political issue earlier in 1992 when it
became known publicly that women are not used as subjects in
many medical trials and that breast cancer research was seriously
underfunded relative to diseases that affect fewer Americans.[86]
The most revealing aspect of the Senate's vote to support breast
cancer research at the expense of the military budget was the fact
that twenty-eight senators who opposed the bill scrambled to make
a last-minute switch to support the winning side when it became
apparent that the military budget would not be protected by a
majority of senators.[87] At the same time, senators were submitting
a flood of new legislation addressing issues of concern to women:
"[H]ardly a day goes by without a Senate vote on an issue of
concern to women, ranging from legislation to guarantee workers
a right to unpaid leave to handle medical emergencies to amend-

ments dealing with pension rights for abused spouses of military personnel."[88]

In news reports concerning senators' sudden interest in the problems of their female constituents, senators and commentators uniformly attributed their actions to the highly publicized Thomas-Hill hearings and the public's political reaction to the Senate's handling of the controversy. Although senators would normally return to their usual interests and pet projects after memories of the Thomas-Hill controversy begin to fade among members of the public, many observers expect the Senate to become increasingly sensitive to women's issues. This sensitivity will not stem from changes in the male senators' values or from their guilt about mishandling Anita Hill's allegations. Instead, the legislative attention to women was expected to come from the presence of more women senators who could use their voices and their votes to keep their male colleagues from ignoring the problems facing the largest demographic group in American society, the female majority.

THE THOMAS NOMINATION AS A
CRITICAL JUDICIAL NOMINATION

The American political landscape changed in the aftermath of the Thomas nomination hearings. The Thomas-Hill hearings mobilized women candidates, contributors, and voters to seek greater representation for women in the U.S. Senate and other government offices. In response, elected officials have paid greater attention to issues of concern to women because of fears that the political forces mobilized in the aftermath of the Thomas nomination would adversely affect the careers of unresponsive politicians. Women ultimately won races for public office at an unprecedented level in the 1992 elections. Five of eleven women candidates won U.S. senate races, 48 of the 106 women candidates won seats in the U.S. House of Representatives, 4 women won victories as states' lieutenant governors and 4 more as states' attorneys general, and women won 20 percent of the seats in state legislatures.[89] Although women candidates and their campaign literature provided explicit confirmation that the Thomas nomination was a catalytic event for women's political mobilization in 1992, several other factors also affected these political developments. First, the electorate's anti-incumbency mood assisted outsider candidates, including women, especially in the aftermath of the massive check bouncing scandal that involved many members of the House of Representatives. Second, the threat to abortion rights posed by the Reagan and Bush appointees to the Supreme Court generated political action by pro-choice women, including many in the affluent and educated demographic groups who were most outraged by Anita Hill's treatment. Third, voters blamed President Bush and the Republicans for the dismal state of the American economy and these sentiments helped the many women candidates who were Democrats. Fourth, because many of the women candidates were experienced politicians who had worked their way through various elective offices, some of their success in 1992 may be attributable to the evolutionary integration of women into electoral politics as American society gradually became more receptive to female leaders and women became more assertive in seeking public office.

In addition to the foregoing factors, the Republicans miscalculated the effects of the Thomas-Hill hearings in developing their campaign strategies. Republican strategists initially believed that the hearings had driven a wedge between the Democrats' traditional constituencies of African-Americans (many of whom supported Thomas) and liberal women (most of whom supported Hill). They hoped that they could emphasize the association between the Democrats and Anita Hill's feminist supporters in order to attract support from larger numbers of African-Americans and from moderate white voters.[90] African-Americans, however, remained loyal to the Democrats[91] and many moderate whites were disturbed by President Bush's ineffectiveness in addressing national economic problems. The Republicans also sought to emphasize "family values" by criticizing Hillary Clinton, the wife of Democratic presidential candidate Bill Clinton, who was a successful attorney and well-known advocate for children's legal rights. Vice-President Dan Quayle and his wife both gave highly publicized speeches that criticized single mothers and appeared to praise stay-at-home-mothers as ideal female role models. Vice-President Quayle criticized fictitious television character Murphy Brown, an unmarried journalist, for choosing to have a baby without a husband.[92] Marilyn Quayle said of Hillary Clinton, for example, "Not everyone [in our generation] believed that the family was so oppressive that women could only thrive apart from it. . . . Most women do not wish to be liberated from their essential nature as women."[93] The Republicans quickly abandoned this strategy because their attacks on people outside of the stereotypical image of the traditional nuclear family only further alienated the educated women mobilized by the Thomas-Hill hearings. Moreover, the attacks also offended a wider range of working women who have jobs because of financial necessity and who do not enjoy the luxurious option available to Marilyn Quayle and Barbara Bush of staying at home full-time to raise children. Republican pollsters found that "the great majority of the public finds the assaults on [Hillary Clinton] insulting, meanspirited and beside the point."[94] A *Newsweek* poll following the Republican convention found that, of those people surveyed who expressed an opinion, many more felt that the Republicans spent too much time attacking Hillary Clinton (52 percent) and feminists (31\percent) than felt that continued attacks were appropriate (6 percent and 11 percent respectively).[95] President Bush compounded the Republicans' problems with women voters by repeatedly vetoing a family leave bill that was long advocated by women's organizations, passed by bi-partisan majorities in Congress, and endorsed by the Democratic Party. The legislation, which was a weaker version of existing policy in most of Europe, would have required companies to give employees up to twelve weeks of unpaid leave for childbirth, adoption, or caring for a sick child or dying parent. In the midst of the general election campaign, the Senate mustered enough votes to override the veto (68–31), but the House of Representatives fell 27 votes short (258–169) of the two-thirds majority needed to override.[96] In sum, Republican campaign strategies directed at women backfired and contributed to the political mobilization in support of Democratic candidates.

In light of the various factors contributing to the political mobilization of women, can it truly be said that the Thomas nomination was the *sine qua non* for political change, as required by Chapter 1's stated definition for critical judicial nominations? Despite the existence of other elements contributing to the political consciousness, mobilization, and success of women, the Thomas nomination was the crucial catalyst for the political developments that followed. For example, the Republicans' unsuccessful family values theme was implemented *after* women's political mobilization had been demonstrated in the senatorial primary elections. Thus this failed strategy merely enhanced rather than initiated the consciousness and mobilization of women voters. In addition, many of the other contributing factors had been in existence to varying degrees in previous elections without having had such a significant impact on electoral politics.

For example, abortion had been a motivating issue for many women in previous elections during the Reagan and Bush presidencies when new Supreme Court justices were appointed who possessed viewpoints that were critical of abortion rights. Prochoice activists mobilized after the Supreme Court's 1989 decision that invited states to regulate, but not ban, abortion.[97] However, as noted in the *Washington Post*'s analysis, "in 1990, the abortion issue was not a deciding factor in most races and the majority of women candidates for statewide office were defeated."[98] In 1992, abortion rights were no more threatened than in the aftermath of the 1989 decision because, despite the presence of Justice Thomas's anti-abortion vote, Justice Anthony Kennedy switched sides to preserve the Court's prohibition against state statutes banning abortion.[99] Thus because the abortion issue remained as much of a motivating factor for many voters in 1992 as it was in 1990, the unique political changes that occurred in 1992, but not in 1990, are actually attributable to the impetus from the Thomas nomination controversy.

The electorate's anti-incumbency mood and the Republican administration's economic problems helped women candidates, but these factors did not provide sufficient motivation to mobilize women candidates and voters. For example, Carol Moseley Braun and Lynn Yeakel entered their respective Senate races because of their feelings about the Thomas-Hill hearings. They would not have run for office without that catalytic event even in a year of strong anti-incumbency sentiments and serious economic problems. Similarly, the financial contributions and electoral support for women candidates would not have been as great without the Thomas nomination controversy. Although women were entering more political races in the 1990s, the surprising and unique success of women candidates in upsetting well-funded and better known male opponents in 1992 primary elections did not depend on the anti-incumbent orientation of voters. Political reactions to the Thomas-Hill hearings propelled women candidates to the forefront in these primary elections which, except for the case of Illinois, did not pit women candidates against the incumbent senators who might have been disadvantaged by anti-incumbency sentiments.

A second and more difficult question that can be posed concerning the classification of the Thomas nomination as critical is whether significant political change in fact occurred in 1992. Increased representation for women in the U.S. Senate still leaves them woefully underrepresented relative to their proportion within the country's population.[100] Despite the limited progress toward equitable representation, however, the election of new officeholders deserves classification as a significant change. This development was something more than a mere temporary mobilization of women voters concerning a particular issue such as abortion or the ERA. Even without achieving proportional representation, by increasing the number of women as speakers, bill proposers, and voters within the halls of governmental power, public policy issues will be shaped, debated, and considered in light of new viewpoints. Unlike other democracies that have had women serve as national leaders (e.g., Great Britain, India, Norway, Iceland, and Israel) or have strong representation by women in national legislatures (e.g., Denmark) and governmental agencies (e.g., Australia),[101] the United States has a long legacy of male monopolization of decision making in policymaking institutions. Developments in 1992 may fall far short of feminists' aspirations for equal gender representation in government. However, the notable increases in women's congressional representation produced in a single election stand in marked contrast to the political history and traditions of the United States. Thus the Thomas nomination controversy can be classified as the catalytic event that generated significant political change.

NOTES

1. Elizabeth Kolbert, "Survey Finds Most of Public Believes Nominee's Account," *N.Y. Times*, 15 October 1991; Jane Mansbridge and Katherine Tate, "Race Trumps Gender: The Thomas Nomination in the Black Community," *P.S.: Political Science and Politics* 25 (1992): 488–92; Kathleen Frankovic and Joyce Gelb, "Public Opinion and the Thomas Nomination," *P.S.: Political Science and Politics* 25 (1992): 481–84.

2. Mansbridge and Tate, "Race Trumps Gender," 491.

3. William Hershey, "Women in Washington Know Reality Behind Thomas-Hill Fiasco," *Akron Beacon Journal*, 21 October 1991, A7.

4. Jill Abramson, "Reversal of Fortune: Image of Anita Hill Brighter in Hindsight, Galvanizes Campaigns," *Wall Street Journal*, 5 October 1992, A1.

5. Saundra Torry, "60% of Female Lawyers Surveyed Report Gender Bias in U.S. Courts," *Akron Beacon Journal*, 6 August 1992, A13.

6. Abramson, "Reversal of Fortune," A1.

7. Ibid.

8. For example, Eleanor Flexner, *Century of Struggle: The Woman's Rights Movement in the United States*, rev. ed. (Cambridge, Mass.: Harvard University Press, 1975).

9. Ethel Klein, *Gender Politics* (Cambridge, Mass.: Harvard University Press, 1984), 13.

10. Ibid., 14–16.

11. Ibid., 16.

12. Ibid., 16–21.

13. Ibid., 150.

14. M. Kent Jennings, "Women in Party Politics," in *Women, Politics, and Change*, eds. Louise A. Tilly and Patricia Gurin (New York: Russell Sage Foundation, 1990), 245.

15. Klein, *Gender Politics*, 154.

16. Ibid., 155.

17. Ibid., 162–63.

18. Ibid., 162.

19. Ibid., 156.

20. Virginia Sapiro, *The Political Integration of Women* (Urbana, Ill.: University of Illinois Press, 1983), 103.

21. Ibid.

22. Judy Mann, "They Don't Just Get Mad," *Washington Post*, 27 March 1992, E3.

23. Arthur Miller, "Gender and the Vote: 1984," in *The Politics of the Gender Gap: The Social Construction of Political Influence*, ed. Carol M. Mueller (Newbury Park, Calif.: Sage Publications, 1988), 258–82.

24. Klein, *Gender Politics*, 161–62.

25. Carol M. Mueller, "The Empowerment of Women: Polling the Women's Voting Bloc," in *The Politics of the Gender Gap: The Social Construction of Political Influence*, ed. Carol M. Mueller (Newbury Park, Calif.: Sage Publications, 1988), 25.

26. Priscilla Painton, "Woman Power," *Time*, 28 October 1991, 24–25.

27. "Dividing Lines," *Newsweek*, 28 October 1991, 24.

28. Susan Page, "U.S. Gender Gap to Narrow," *Akron Beacon Journal*, 22 September 1992, A2.

29. Todd S. Purdum, "Primary in Hand, Abrams Sets Out to Oust D'Amato," *N.Y. Times*, 17 September 1992, A12.

30. Page, "U.S. Gender Gap to Narrow," A2.

31. Isabel Wilkerson, "Illinois Senator Is Defeated by County Politician," *N.Y. Times*, 18 March 1992, A19.

32. Isabel Wilkerson, "Storming Senate 'Club'," *N.Y. Times*, 19 March 1992, A20.

33. Ibid.

34. Ibid.

35. "Illinois Vote Sounds Alarm for Incumbents," *N.Y. Times*, 19 March 1992, A20.

36. Ibid.

37. Maralee Schwartz and Lauren Ina, "Senate Upset Reflects Powerful Legacy of Thomas Hearings," *Washington Post*, 19 March 1992, A15.

38. Abramson, "Reversal of Fortune," A4.

39. Frank James, "Braun Hits the Streets to say 'Thanks': Her Gratitude Goes Out to a Wide Spectrum of Voters," *Chicago Tribune*, 5 November 1992.

40. Thomas Hardy, "Braun Rode Colorblind Coalition," *Chicago Tribune*, 8 November 1992.

41. Dale Russakoff, "An 'Outsider' Triumphs Again," *Washington Post*, 29 April 1992.

42. Ibid., A1.

43. Dale Russakoff, "Senate Nominee Yeakel Thanks Pennsylvanians," *Washington Post*, 30 April 1992, A17.

44. Russakoff, "An 'Outsider' Triumphs Again," A1.

45. Michael deCourcy Hinds, "After Making Specter the Issue, Newcomer Wins Bid to Face Him," *N.Y. Times*, 29 April 1992, A19.

46. Ibid.

47. Abramson, "Reversal of Fortune," A1.

48. Ibid., A4.

49. Nathan Gorenstein, "Specter Defeats Yeakel," *Philadelphia Inquirer*, 4 November 1992, 1.

50. Nathan Gorenstein, "A Verdict on Yeakel: She Could Have Had It," *Philadelphia Inquirer*, 8 November 1992, E2.

51. Ibid.

52. Nathan Gorenstein, "Specter's Strategy Takes Him Back to U.S. Senate," *Philadelphia Inquirer*, 5 November 1992, A16.

53. "California's Double-Barreled Senate Race," *N.Y. Times*, 11 April 1992, 8.

54. Jane Gross, "Strategies Emerge in Dual Senate Races," *N.Y. Times*, 11 April 1992, 8.

55. Timothy M. Phelps and Helen Winternitz, *Capitol Games* (New York: Hyperion, 1992), 426–27.

56. Dean E. Murphy and Tracy Wilkinson, "Feinstein Off to Job, Boxer Takes Break," *Los Angeles Times*, 5 November 1992, 1; Patt

Morrison, "A Solid 'Year of the Woman' at State Polls," *Los Angeles Times*, 5 November 1992.

57. Lou Cannon, "Women Triumph in California Senate Contests," *Washington Post*, 3 June 1992.

58. Ibid., A14.

59. Gross, "Strategies Emerge," 8.

60. Maureen Dowd, "7 House Women March to Senate in Attempt to Delay Thomas Vote," *N.Y. Times*, 9 October 1991, A1.

61. Ibid.

62. Margaret Carlson, "The Ultimate Men's Club," *Time*, 21 October 1991, 51.

63. Dowd, "7 House Women March," A1.

64. "California's Double-Barreled Senate Race," 8.

65. Maralee Schwartz, "A Flash Flood, or A Mighty Stream?" *Washington Post National Weekly Edition*, 21–27 October 1991, 14.

66. Murphy and Wilkinson, "Feinstein Off to Job," 1.

67. Timothy Egan, "Another Win, By a Woman, This One 'Mom'," *N.Y. Times*, 17 September 1992, A8.

68. Ibid.

69. Abramson, "Reversal of Fortune," A1.

70. Rebecca Boren, "Murray Wins Senate Seat by Big Margin," *Seattle Post-Intelligencer*, 4 November 1992.

71. "Women: A Revolution Sweeping the Country," *Democrats*, Summer 1992, 4.

72. Schwartz, "A Flash Flood," 14.

73. Abramson, "Reversal of Fortune," A4.

74. Phelps and Winternitz, *Capitol Games*, 427.

75. "$16 Million Is New Record for Democrats," *Akron Beacon Journal*, 1 September 1992, A3.

76. Mann, "They Don't Just Get Mad," E3.

77. Fox Butterfield, "2 Women Defy Odds in New Hampshire Governor's Race," *N.Y. Times*, 5 September 1992, 5.

78. Mueller, "The Empowerment of Women," 25.

79. "Overheard," *Newsweek*, 31 August 1992, 25.

80. Quoted in *Akron Beacon Journal*, 26 September 1992, A2.

81. Karen Schneider, "Women Find Politics Gets Nasty, Personal: Finally Playing in the Big Leagues, Many Candidates Must Take Time to Confront Lies about Private Lives," *Akron Beacon Journal*, 19 September 1992, A5.

82. Ibid.

83. Ibid.

84. Neil A. Lewis, "Court Nominee Is Confirmed After Angry Senate Debate," *N.Y. Times*, 10 September 1992, A8.

85. Helen Dewar, "Senate Gets the Message: Pay Attention to Women," *Akron Beacon Journal*, 24 September 1992, A1.

86. Mann, "They Don't Just Get Mad," E3.

87. Dewar, "Senate Gets the Message," A1.

88. Ibid., A11.

89. Patt Morrison, "Women Assess the Spoils of Victory," *Los Angeles Times*, 6 November 1992, 3; Meg Dennison, "Women Bring Agendas to State Legislatures," *Akron Beacon Journal*, 19 November 1992, A3.

90. Ann Devroy, "The GOP Makes Hay Out of the Hearings," *Washington Post National Weekly Edition*, 28 October–3 November 1991, 8.

91. Jonathan Tilove, "Candidates Have Different Histories, Outlooks on Race," *Cleveland Plain Dealer*, 27 September 1992, 10–A.

92. Richard Zoglin, "Sitcom Politics," *Time*, 21 September 1992, 44.

93. Margaret Carlson, "All Eyes on Hillary," *Time*, 14 September 1992, 31.

94. Ibid., 32.

95. "Bush: What Bounce?" *Newsweek*, 31 August 1992, 29.

96. William J. Eaton, "House Unable to Override Veto of Family-Leave Bill," *Akron Beacon Journal*, 1 October 1992, A16.

97. Webster v. Reproductive Health Services, 109 S. Ct. 3040 (1989).

98. Schwartz, "A Flash Flood," 14.

99. Planned Parenthood v. Casey, 112 S. Ct. 2791 (1992). *See also* Christopher E. Smith, "Supreme Court Surprise: Justice Anthony Kennedy's Move Toward Moderation," *Oklahoma Law Review* 45 (1992): 459–76.

100. Hester Eisenstein, "Scholars in Women's Studies Can Help Put This Fall's Elections Into Perspective," *The Chronicle of Higher Education*, 23 September 1992, B1.

101. Ibid., B2.

6

Conclusion

When George Bush nominated Clarence Thomas to replace retiring Justice Thurgood Marshall on the Supreme Court, most observers expected that combative confirmation hearings would pit liberal senators against their conservative colleagues in, respectively, challenging and defending Judge Thomas's qualifications and judicial philosophy. Most observers also expected Thomas to be confirmed with modest opposition as long as he did not make any mistakes during the confirmation hearings. Thomas's relatively weak performance before the Committee softened his potential support as the Committee deadlocked 7–7 when voting on whether to endorse his nomination. Despite opposition from most Democratic members of the Judiciary Committee, Thomas was poised to win his confirmation vote with the support of several Democratic senators and thereby assume his position as the Court's newest appointee. Up to that point, the Thomas nomination was simply another nomination that divided liberals and conservatives who were concerned about the immediate future of Supreme Court decision making. However, when Professor Anita Hill's charges of sexual harassment against Thomas emerged and the Judiciary Committee failed to either thoroughly investigate the charges or give her a fair, respectful hearing, the Thomas nomination was transformed into a catalytic political event that generated important consequences for the mobilization of women candidates and voters. Public reactions to the male-dominated Senate's inability to understand Hill's plausible allegations of sexual harassment affected electoral behavior and outcomes in the 1992 election.

It might be possible to view the Thomas nomination and its aftermath as an isolated incident generated by unique circumstances. From the perspective of a political scientist, however, such important developments in the political system must be examined with consideration for the possibility that the Thomas nomination and other judicial nominations are not unique events. Certainly, each judicial nomination is different. The individual actors involved and the particular moment in political history when each nomination is made obviously differ with every presidential decision about who will fill a vacancy on the Supreme Court. However, because the federal judicial nomination process embodies such an important intersection point for the interactions of the various branches of government, there may be patterns or shared characteristics discernible in the processes or consequences of judicial nominations.

The Thomas nomination had evident consequences for the American political system. Although the precise impact of this nomination, namely the mobilization of female candidates and voters, was distinctive, the fact that the nomination had important consequences for the political system was not unique. Other judicial nominations have produced important effects on various aspects of the political system, too. Thus, the foregoing chapters of this book have endeavored to develop a concept (i.e., critical judicial nominations) that can assist scholars in classifying the Thomas nomination and other nominations that produce significant consequences for the political system.

The examples discussed in this book focused on two primary consequences of specific judicial nominations. The Thomas nomination illustrated the impact of a critical nomination on electoral behavior and outcomes. The examples in Chapter 2 concerning John Marshall, Earl Warren, and Abe Fortas illustrated the impact that specific nominations have on the role of the Supreme Court in the political system. These are not, however, the only kinds of important political consequences that may be produced by critical judicial nominations. A nomination might, for example, mobilize interest groups and change their relationships with each other. When President Reagan unsuccessfully nominated Judge Robert Bork for a seat on the Supreme Court in 1987, dozens of liberal and conservative interest groups organized to mount public relations campaigns that would, respectively, oppose and support the Bork nomination.[1] The mobilization of interest groups also occurred in response to other Supreme Court nominations, including Louis Brandeis's nomination in 1916 and John J. Parker's unsuccessful nomination in 1930.[2] If, in the course of focusing attention on a judicial nomination, interest groups formed new coalitions and continuing relationships that subsequently affected their political power on other issues, that nomination, whether or not successful, might deserve classification as a critical judicial nomination. Indeed, the Republicans initially hoped that the Thomas nomination would drive a wedge between feminist interest groups and African-American interest groups and thereby make African-American voters more supportive of Republican candidates.[3] Although the Thomas nomination did not ultimately produce an enduring schism between these traditional Democratic constituencies, such important political developments could be generated by judicial nominations.

The examples in this book are not meant to limit criteria for assessing the important political consequences of judicial nominations. Instead, the concept of critical judicial nominations is intended to create a useful tool for considering broadly whether judicial nominations have discernible impacts beyond simply the Supreme Court's immediate case decisions that will be produced when specific new appointees join the highest court. Presumably the Supreme Court's role and importance in the American governing system can be better understood through recognition of all of the judicial branch's impacts on the political system. Although judicial decisions and their impact on public policy, government, and society are the most well-recognized and thoroughly studied aspects of the Supreme Court's role, the judicial nomination process represents another useful focal point for discerning the importance of judicial institutions as influential components of the political system.

As scholars continue to debate the Supreme Court's importance as a policy-making institution,[4] there is a risk that a preoccupation with questions about judicial policy making will obscure recognition of other judicial impacts that may produce important consequences through less direct means. By reorienting assessments of the Supreme Court's history and role away from the Court's prevalent image as a policy-making institution, the concept of critical judicial nominations provides a classification mechanism for seeking to recognize less obvious and less direct political consequences of an important, judicial focused intersection for interactions between the branches of government. Whether or not other scholars ultimately conclude that, as a classification tool, the critical judicial nomination concept is properly defined and effective for its stated purpose, the concept should be useful as a focal point for analyses and discussions that seek understanding of the judicial branch's broader, less direct, and less recognized impact and importance for the American political system.

NOTES

1. David M. O'Brien, *Storm Center: The Supreme Court in American Politics*, 2d ed. (New York: W. W. Norton, 1990), 106–11.

2. Gregory A. Caldeira and John R. Wright, "Lobbying for Justice: Organized Interests Before the Senate, 1916–90," *VOX POP: Newsletter of Political Organizations and Parties* 10 (1991): 4–5; Gregory A. Caldeira and John R. Wright, "Lobbying for Justice: The Rise of Organized Conflict in the Politics of Federal Judgeships." Paper presented at the annual meeting of the American Political Science Association, 1990.

3. Ann Devroy, "GOP Makes Hay Out of the Hearings," *Washington Post National Weekly Edition*, 28 October–3 November 1991, 8; Thomas B. Edsall and E.J. Dionne, Jr., "The Vote That Split the Liberal Core: Blacks and Feminists Were Miles Apart on Thomas," *Washington Post National Weekly Edition*, 21–27 October 1991, 12.

4. For example, Gerald Rosenberg, *The Hollow Hope: Can Courts Bring About Social Change?* (Chicago: University of Chicago Press, 1991).

Select Bibliography

Abraham, Henry J. *Justices and Presidents: A Political History of Appointments to the Supreme Court*, 2d ed. New York: Oxford University Press, 1985.

Baum, Lawrence. *The Supreme Court*. 4th ed. Washington, D.C.: Congressional Quarterly Press, 1992.

Bodenhamer, David J. *Fair Trial: Rights of the Accused in American History*. New York: Oxford University Press, 1992.

Bumiller, Kristin. "Victims in the Shadow of the Law: A Critique of the Model of Legal Protection." *Signs: Journal of Women in Culture and Society* 12 (1987): 421–39.

Burnham, Walter Dean. *Critical Elections and the Mainsprings of American Politics*. New York: W. W. Norton, 1970.

Cox, Archibald. *The Court and the Constitution*. Boston: Houghton Mifflin, 1987.

Douglas, William O. *The Court Years, 1939–1975*. New York: Random House, 1980.

Felstiner, William L. F., Richard L. Abel, and Austin Sarat. "The Emergence and Transformation of Disputes: Naming, Blaming, Claiming. . . ." *Law and Society Review* 15 (1980–81): 631–54.

Frankel, Marvin. *Partisan Justice*. New York: Hill & Wang, 1978.

Frankovic, Kathleen, and Joyce Gelb. "Public Opinion and the Thomas Nomination." *P.S.: Political Science & Politics* 25 (1992): 481–84.

Galanter, Marc. "Reading the Landscape of Disputes: What We Know and Don't Know (and Think We Know) About Our Allegedly Contentious and Litigious Society." *U.C.L.A. Law Review* 31 (1983): 4–71.

Jaros, Dean, and Robert Roper. "The U.S. Supreme Court: Myth, Diffuse Support, Specific Support, and Legitimacy." *American Politics Quarterly* 8 (1980): 85–105.

Johnson, Scott P., and Christopher E. Smith. "David Souter's First Term on the Supreme Court: The Impact of a New Justice." *Judicature* 75 (1992): 238–43.

Kalman, Laura. *Abe Fortas*. New Haven, Conn: Yale University Press, 1990.

Key, V. O., Jr. "A Theory of Critical Elections." *Journal of Politics* 17 (1955): 2–18.

Klein, Ethel. *Gender Politics*. Cambridge, Mass.: Harvard University Press, 1984.

Mansbridge, Jane, and Katherine Tate. "Race Trumps Gender: The Thomas Nomination in the Black Community." *P.S.: Political Science & Politics* 25 (1992): 488–92.

Massaro, John. "LBJ and the Fortas Nomination for Chief Justice." *Political Science Quarterly* 97 (1982–83): 603–21.

Melone, Albert P., Alan R. Morris, and Marc-George Pufong. "Too Little Advice, Senatorial Responsibility, and Confirmation Politics." *Judicature* 75 (1992): 187–92, 228.

Miller, Richard E., and Austin Sarat. "Grievances, Claims, and Disputes: Assessing the Adversary Culture." *Law and Society Review* 15 (1980–81): 525–66.

Mueller, Carol M., ed. *The Politics of the Gender Gap: The Social Construction of Political Influence*. Newbury Park, Calif.: Sage Publications, 1988.

Murphy, Bruce Allen. *Fortas: The Rise and Ruin of a Supreme Court Justice*. New York: William Morrow, 1988.

Newmyer, R. Kent. *The Supreme Court under Marshall and Taney*. Arlington Heights, Ill.: Harlan Davidson, 1968.

O'Brien, David. *Storm Center: The Supreme Court in American Politics*, 2d ed. New York: W. W. Norton, 1990.

O'Connor, Karen. "The Effects of the Thomas Appointment to the Supreme Court." *P.S.: Political Science & Politics* 25 (1992): 492–95.

Phelps, Timothy M., and Helen Winternitz. *Capitol Games.* New York: Hyperion, 1992.

Rosenberg, Gerald. *The Hollow Hope.* Chicago: University of Chicago Press, 1991.

Sapiro, Virginia. *The Political Integration of Women.* Urbana, Ill.: University of Illinois Press, 1983.

Schwartz, Herman. *Packing the Courts: The Conservative Campaign to Rewrite the Constitution.* New York: Charles Scribner's Sons, 1988.

Shafer, Byron E., ed. *The End of Realignment?: Interpreting American Electoral Eras.* Madison, Wis.: University of Wisconsin Press, 1991.

Smith, Christopher E. *Courts and the Poor.* Chicago: Nelson-Hall, 1991.

Smith, Christopher E., and Scott P. Johnson. "Newcomer on the High Court: Justice Souter and the Supreme Court's 1990 Term." *South Dakota Law Review* 37 (1992): 21–43.

Thomas, Virginia Lamp. "Breaking Silence." *People,* 11 November 1991, 108–16.

Tilly, Louise A., and Patricia Gurin, eds. *Women, Politics, and Change.* New York: Russell Sage Foundation, 1990.

Urofsky, Melvin I. *A March of Liberty: A Constitutional History of the United States.* New York: Alfred A. Knopf, 1988.

White, G. Edward. *The American Judicial Tradition.* Rev. ed. New York: Oxford University Press, 1988.

_____. *The Marshall Court and Cultural Change, 1815–1835.* New York: Oxford University Press, 1991.

Index

About the Author

CHRISTOPHER E. SMITH is Associate Professor of Political Science at the University of Akron in Ohio. He is the author of seven books on the judiciary including *United States Magistrates in the Federal Courts* (Praeger, 1990) and *Justice Antonin Scalia and the Supreme Court's Conservative Moment* (Praeger, forthcoming, 1994).